C000242977

Losing Tom.

Finding Grace

Jackie Slough

Copyright 2011 © Jackie Slough

Onwards and Upwards Publishers Ltd
Berkeley House
11 Nightingale Crescent
West Horsley
Surrey
KT24 6PD
England

www.onwardsandupwards.org

ISBN: 978-1-907509-07-0

The right of Jackie Slough to be identified as the author of this work has been asserted by her in accordance with the Copyright, Designs and Patents Act 1988.

All rights reserved.

No part of this publication may be reproduced or transmitted in any form or by any means, electronic or mechanical, including photocopy, recording or any information storage and retrieval system, without permission in writing from the author or publisher.

Cover design: Ana Marissa

Printed in the UK

FOREWORD

How can a book written about a story of pain and sadness be such a positive book? It seems almost impossible to think that one would finish reading this story and come away uplifted and encouraged.

That's how we felt as we turned the pages of Jackie's journal. We seemed to enter the very emotional struggles with her and Alan, but left with a sense of peace and hope. But then it's not really surprising because Jackie's prayer, recorded towards the end of the journal, is for "everyone who reads it to be touched by the glory of God". We found that prayer answered.

We feel privileged to be asked to write this foreword because although we know Jackie and Alan, and have walked with them from a distance and occasionally more closely through this journey, we have been able to share so much more, through the prose and poetry, of the painful pathway with its twists and turns; its rocky stretches and more gentle yards.

It is such a down-to-earth, real story of how Jackie and Alan, and James, have lived with the tragedy of Tom's suicide. Nothing seems to be hidden; you can feel the anguish, the bouts of guilt, the searching, unanswerable questions, the positive times when the strength of friendship and sense of God's presence and comfort provides a realistic foundation for a future and a hope. Jackie has been so expressive in her openness and honesty that we often found ourselves thinking, "Oh, I can see how you'd feel like that", or, "Yes, of course, it must be like that" – and we had no right to because, although we've been through our own problems, we have not lived with that kind of tragic loss. We felt that Jackie was sharing just with us.

How very helpful this book is for anyone going through the grief of loss. You will feel understood, not alone, helped and strengthened. Read it anyway because, even if you haven't experienced this level of suffering, you will begin to understand, and you will find yourself strangely warmed and enriched as you realise afresh that God's help and comfort and, indeed, his grace are not a figment of the imagination, but a rock-solid reality.

Rob & Marion White
December 2010

Introduction

This book has been a long time in the making and there have been many times when I could easily have thrown it away, when I have thought it rubbish and not worth the paper it is written on, but Alan always encouraged me to think otherwise – even though he had not read it, except for the poems. Many times it has seemed like someone else's story and yet I know it is mine, all the thoughts, feelings and things we went through were all real and were written down as they happened or as best as I could remember them.

I never really knew what would become of it, although I felt it was to be of benefit to others, but God has His plans for it and He wouldn't let it go. Each time I was knocked back or discouraged and decided not to go ahead with it and that it was written purely as a healing thing for me, God would turn it around and bring me into contact with someone to encourage me and to make it happen and be the book you are holding now. I pray you are blessed. I pray you are moved. I pray you know Jesus a little bit more by the end of it, or at least, that you want to know him more, and that you know how much you are loved and valued by our God. I pray that in some small or significant way that your life will be changed because of it. God bless. See you later!

Dedicated to Tom

Acknowledgements

I want to **thank all the people who have carried us in their hearts** and prayed for us for the last seven years, especially those from **Chipping Campden Baptist Church** and the other **Cornerstone Churches.**

Thanks to all those who have encouraged me to continue with this book.

Special **thanks to Rev'd Philip Deller who has walked with us** every step and without whose love and friendship I would not be here and Alan and I would not be the strength that we are. **Thanks to God for His amazing love and grace**, which He has lavished upon us and which, is where the title for this book came from.

Before Friday 30th January 2004

I realised Tom was going through a tough time – 16, hormones and girls; and thought his music taste and general behaviour was something he had to go through and would come through and use to help others.

He knew I didn't approve of the music and his apparent hero worship of Kurt Cobain and Nirvana but his arguments were always constructive and I could see where he was coming from – as he could my concerns. He was still helpful and the 'normal' Tom and we had no reason to suspect anything deeper. We respected his opinion on the decorating and planned and took interest in 'A level' plans etc. He was probably coming to Romania with the Church group; was looking forward to a CYFA Christian youth camp reunion on Saturday (the next day...) and the same group's youth camp at Sparkford in the summer; and we had absolutely no idea of what was in his head.

We'd had a lovely Christmas – he said the best ever! (Was that because he knew it would be his last...?) It was relaxed and just the four of us; we were home from church after two, had a light lunch, opened presents (read, *"The Night before Christmas"* because I'd forgotten it the night before – I was so tired and in bed and asleep at 9:30pm); ate dinner late and watched T.V. – a lovely normal Christmas! We all said it was the best! We'd gone from the service to the pub and back to Phil and Hermey's, our Minister and his wife, so James (our oldest son) could install a computer program for their daughter, Caris, which was why we were so late home.

After Christmas – mid-January – Tom had marks on his neck. I asked him about them and he said they were from the cross that he wore. It had been too tight while he slept. I thought it was odd but I believed him – who wouldn't when there were no other clues around?

He came home raving about History 'A level' and we discussed several times whether he should do Law as an option or English; we felt English was better, given his natural talent – he could do Law at 'Uni' if he still wanted to. The Law idea came from a friend who wanted to do Law as a career and was trying to get a course started at school – if enough students were interested something might have been set up.

Tom had been to three music gigs held monthly for teenagers in Moreton: the first, he met his girlfriend, the second, he got drunk because he and his girlfriend had split up – we heard him come home and go straight upstairs. When he didn't come down, we went up to find him almost comatose over the loo, so we called an ambulance because he said his drink had been spiked. (And we believed him – who wouldn't – our Tom didn't lie…) but he confessed to the paramedics that he'd taken drink from our cupboards. (We discovered weeks later that he had refilled the bottles with water.) When we got home, from the hospital, I stayed up with him making him drink water. He was almost unconscious, on the kitchen floor, he had drunk so much. Eventually I got him to bed. He couldn't or wouldn't tell us why he had done that but we thought he'd learnt a valuable lesson and we did not need to punish him in any way– except to send him to work the next day!

At the third gig, a boy and girl, two of Tom's friends, got arrested for smoking drugs – the girl was the only one smoking it; the boy was arrested because he was with her. Tom was really there for his friend, offering support to his mum, saying it was not something her son would do. It was a really supportive time for that group of friends. Tom and I talked freely with each other about drugs and friendships and I praised Tom for the support he was giving his friends. We were really proud of him, after the last gig, and felt he had redeemed himself and regained our trust.

Tom had had two class discussions at school about his faith, one in November, during History, with three friends. He said they had asked tough questions but he'd handled it well. The debate was allowed to go on by the teacher, who was impressed by the depth and maturity of the discussion. (She mentioned this to us at Parents' Evening.) The second time was a much bigger affair – at least ten friends, all with real tough questions. Tom came home drained, physically and mentally, but fired up as well. He said he had prayed through the whole time and drew strength and his answers from God – it really deepened his own faith and belief. You could tell he knew, with conviction, what he had shared with his friends and it was so good and Bible based.

I had worried that Tom was slipping away from God – not coming to church on Sunday evenings and doing the computer and junior church every other Sunday, when he wasn't working – always giving out and not necessarily receiving. He knew I was worried. We'd talked about it, along with my concerns about his taste in music. We'd talked about spiritual warfare and how Satan would use anything bad and wrap it up to look good, to take him away from Jesus. We had to agree to disagree about the music aspect but I believed he would come through and times like the big debate at school made me think he would be okay. He would come through and go on to do great things for God – within ministry, perhaps, in the years ahead. That was my own personal thought and not something I shared with Tom. I didn't want him to feel pressured.

Friday 30th January 2004

I woke with a start at 7:26am – I am usually up just after 7:00am. I woke James. He was late too and I went to wake Tom. I was surprised to find him already dressed for school and putting on his socks or shoes – can't remember which. We looked at each other, I thought, in surprise – me at finding him dressed when I'd had to wake him and call him several times each day for weeks (late nights I thought!) but I was grateful because he could start the dogs off for me (we owned several Border Collies, most of which lived outside in a kennel with run, and needed to be let out each morning) and put the kettle on etc. while I washed my hair. I remember an 'odd' look on his face but took it to be at my surprise. I can't remember saying, *"Bye,"* when he went to school but I'd gone out to clean the dogs run – we probably said, *"See you later."* It was just another 'normal' day...

Alan had finished work early (he was an HGV driver for a distribution company) and came to the teashop where I worked, to pick me up and give me a lift home. We stayed chatting with Bev and Paul, my bosses and the owners of the shop, so we got home just after 5:30pm. I went upstairs to the loo and then got changed. Tom's music was playing quite loud but no louder than usual when he did homework and his door was shut. I was looking forward to a whole weekend off. I was ready for it and I was tired. I remember, at some point, finishing up at work feeling very sad and wanting to cry – I assumed it was because I was tired and ready for the weekend. I knew it wasn't my hormones (that's for Alan!). In hindsight, I wonder if, because of the timing, it was Tom and God touching my heart. It was a peaceful feeling even though I did not understand it at the time – anyway enough of fanciful thinking! Once home and changed I wanted to get through as much washing as possible before Sunday, to give me an easy day and not the usual Sunday rush with housework as well as church and everything we tried to fit in.

I knocked on Tom's door and opened – or tried to open it but something was stopping it. I pushed harder and it opened about two inches. I saw Tom sitting on the floor, his back against the wall by the side of the door. I put my hand through, thinking he'd just sat there to listen to his music and that he'd fallen asleep – his head was slightly down and he looked peaceful. I shook his shoulder to wake him. I still couldn't get my hand in any further – didn't know why – there was no response so I shook harder – then I started to shout for Alan. He came racing upstairs, forced the door and told me to call 999. They were brilliant. I was hysterical but they told me what to tell Alan to do; only he was already doing it.

The music was still blaring; it was awful; we knew it was too late. I ran down and opened the door for the paramedics so they could come straight in, and ran back upstairs to the phone. The lady told me how to tell Alan to do chest compressions. I yelled at him to turn the music off. You could tell it was too late for Tom.

The paramedics came and took over in Tom's room; one of them was the same one who'd been out to us when Tom was drunk. Alan came into our room with letters from Tom. We read the one to us; he told us not to cry; it wasn't our fault; and it was to do with things in his head that he couldn't deal with any longer. He said, "See you later," because he knew where he'd gone; and where we're all going; and that we will see each other later.

Then the phone rang. It was James, just saying he was leaving work in Cheltenham. I told him to, "pray, drive carefully and come home, it's Tom." Under the circumstances that was very restrained for me!

Alan tried to phone Philip. It was engaged so I was the one who got through and told Phil – "Tom's dead" – a horrible moment for Phil. I remember he just said, "No!!" – I don't remember any more but he came immediately. (We found out later that as soon as he left the Manse, Hermey set up a prayer chain around the church members.) I rang Mum and Dad; how do you tell your parents? I just said, "Tom's dead"… I rang Bev at work because I knew I wouldn't be in on Monday (surreal thoughts). She said, "I'm coming," and put the phone down, not knowing where we lived. (She found us easily because the ambulance was outside). Things like that have kept us laughing when we probably should have been weeping but God knows our hearts were empty.

Anyway, Bev came first, then Helen our best friend and a wise and wonderful lady of God – we didn't tell her over the phone what had happened. I whispered, in her ear in the hallway, and then looked into her shocked eyes and said, "I need to know because of what he's done; that he's where he thought he was going."

Helen said, "Yes, definitely."

Then Philip came; and then my Mum and Dad; and lots of police at different levels; our G.P. – as the police doctor on call; then James came home.

Alan and I were upstairs with Tom, saying goodbye – I kept saying, "Silly boy, silly, silly boy," but I kissed his forehead as I would do when he was asleep in bed – a very tender moment. We prayed – there was so much peace in our hearts; all his hurt was gone. We couldn't explain that in a way we weren't surprised – Alan, at what he'd done – me, that he'd gone back to God. It was a deep, deep peace so we weren't with the others in the kitchen when they found out what he'd done. Everyone had supposed it was an accident, road or otherwise. The doctor was on the phone, in the hall, and everyone in the kitchen heard him say, 'Suicide." I'm sorry they found out like that but how could we have told them?

So then everyone knew and it was shock, disbelief, desperate tears, hugging and holding, making tea – endless tea. I remember Phil saying, "Tom was a monkey because he was already with Jesus and we weren't," (but that's not the way to see Jesus, we know that). We prayed for the release of his soul, for ourselves and mainly stood around the kitchen, me going from Alan to James, to Mum and Dad, giving a hug and being strong for them. We went upstairs, with James, so he could say goodbye. He felt very angry with Tom and wanted to shake him but we prayed again and went downstairs. Mum and Dad also went up and said their goodbyes.

The undertaker came and took Tom away. I didn't know how I'd cope when they took him, but thankfully I didn't know until afterwards.

The police finally left and Mum and Dad went home. Helen went down into town for some chips, which we shared between Helen, Philip and us. I only ate about three. Helen went home and we sent Phil home – for his sake (and Hermey's) as it was about 11.00pm.

Then we went to bed – I suppose at about 11:30pm – it just seemed the natural thing to do – what else would we have done? It might seem strange to some people that we did, but there was peace in the house and we were tired. James had half a diazepam, which we found in a cupboard, and he slept well. I thought I would sleep because I was so tired. Alan slept – his back to me all night; I know he was comfortable and needed to sleep. I tossed and turned – and a night had never been so long – and I've never longed for morning so much.

Saturday 31st January 2004

Numb and unreal and yet knowing it was real; that's how I felt when I finally got up and that's how Saturday passed, along with a constant stream of visitors and flowers. Philip, Mum, Dad, my sister, a few people from church, some we saw and some we didn't. I remember Tom's friend, Matt, came.

Our doctor came, as our G.P, not as the police doctor. He was lovely. We had to know so we asked for the details of how Tom died – what he would have felt; how long it would have taken. He told us truthfully that Tom wouldn't have felt any pain, that he would have slipped into unconsciousness very quickly and that it was one of the most peaceful deaths in that situation that he had seen. We're grateful for that. We believe that, in his desperation, Tom reached up to Jesus and Jesus took his hand and his pain.

I remember the Deputy Head, from school, came in the morning and came back in the afternoon with phone numbers of Tom's friends and with Tom's Record of Achievement (something each Year 11 students receives before their GCSE's) and his school photo. I put the photo in the cupboard alcove, with flowers and cards, and it's a good place for it, a lovely photo. I remember telling Tom to wash his hair and to do his shirt button up when they took it. He came home saying he didn't think it was going to be good but it's so Tom – big, deep, brown eyes looking into your soul. It's a lovely photo!

I can't remember much more of Saturday. Some more of his friends came. I remember we felt so desperately for them. They were so brave to come and it was so good that they did. Late afternoon, we received the letters, that Tom had written to us, back from the police, and we read some more, and felt Tom's pain and understood a bit more.

Daniel, the Minister from Stour Valley Baptist Church (which was planted from our church in 1999), and who was a blessing to James, came over in the afternoon, drank tea and was just 'there'. He stayed with James, while Alan and I walked the dogs and blew some cobwebs away. We shared a special prayer time – all crying together and we went up into Tom's room and prayed and cried in there too. Dan left.

James and I took a sleeping tablet each (from the doctor this time!). It was good to go straight to sleep and wake up in the morning – even if it was early. Alan didn't need a tablet, he slept anyway.

Sunday 1st February 2004

Church – where else would we go; to whom else would we run? We had planned, with Phil, that it might be best to arrive at 10:25am so there would be the usual bustle and we could go in relatively un-noticed; Helen was saving five chairs; Mum and Dad came with us.

We were doing okay until we met a lady walking down the path to the church, with her family and so we had a hug and a weep with her. We went down the side passage to come in through the front doors and as we passed the patio windows we could see the worship group had stopped playing and we realised there was no music – or children running about; heads seemed to be bowed.

We got to the front doors and Alan nearly couldn't go in; luckily there were still people behind trying to get in so he had to. As we walked to our seats, in the middle of the church, you could feel the church's grief – our pain was their pain.

Philip started the service with the 23rd Psalm. When he got to the 'valley of the shadow of death' he nearly couldn't go on but it gave others permission to be real too. I felt I had to be strong for Alan and James and I felt I had to worship like never before. If people saw me looking to the Lord, they too would turn to Him and praise His name; it was hard, but God is amazing and gave me strength.

As a church, we were working our way through Luke's gospel and had reached chapter 13:22 about 'The Narrow Door'. Philip had wondered whether he should change the message that he had prepared but he felt it right to go with it and it was very appropriate and powerful for the circumstances. The Narrow Door is Jesus himself. Someone asks Him, "Will only a few be saved?" and Jesus answered, "Will you be saved?" Phil went on to say, "Tom may have filled his mind with all sorts of things but one thing he had was a certainty of his destination, even in death, even in taking his life, he knew where he was going and Jesus asks the same question of you, 'Do you know where you are going?'"

As the service progressed, the tangible grief turned to tangible love and peace, which we three each felt in our hearts and knew it felt right. Mum and Dad felt it too; God was reaching down to each of us and pouring His love upon us as a church family.

We had said to Mum and Dad that we would leave the service promptly at the end but that one or two people might want to speak to us on the way out – it never got that far. Kate Barry launched herself (I love you Kate for that memory!) upon Alan and that was how it went on, people queuing to hug us and share our grief. Hermey brought a tray of tea and coffee – mine was cold when I got to it! I'd turn to get it and there'd be someone else who wanted to comfort and show their love for us; people all say we're amazing, but they are the amazing ones; all we've done is cling to the peace God has given us and the certainty that Tom is with Him.

As usual, we were last out of church – poor Mum and Dad! Home to a pre-cooked casserole – thanks Mum!

At about 2:45pm, the Headmaster and Deputy Head arrived, along with two teachers – Tom's 'Head of Year' and another. I had been apprehensive about their visit and was not looking forward to it but it was a good time. They saw our faith and our strength and I think it gave them strength; they've never had to face this before either. They asked what we wanted and what we wanted them to say to the kids in the morning. They gave us good advice about giving a press release and photo and not saying anything else to the press. The school have been brilliant and have helped the kids enormously. We know it was God's hand that stopped school counsellors going into school on the Monday and enabling church people to be there but we didn't tell that to the Head on Sunday when he was cross; he had to leave a message on the counsellor's answer phone! I was even brave enough to tell them all as they left that we'd be praying for them in the morning!

After they'd gone, Matt and some other boys came. I can't remember who, but they were all wet – they'd seen the teachers' cars and waited in the rain around the corner 'till they'd gone'! It was a good time with them, sharing Tom's faith (and our faith), and just to be able to hug them on the way out – they needed that and we were blessed to give.

Sunday evening and back to Church. Again, where else would we go? It's who we are and what we do! It was a good service and a good place to be; James sat a couple of rows behind with his friends, which was good for him. Daniel was leading the service and he spoke on God's love and during the prayer time God spoke of His love for us.

I had asked two questions of God, in the very early hours of Sunday morning – to know with *certainty* that Tom is with Him and to <u>KNOW</u> of His love for us. The first was answered in the morning by Philip's own conviction and the second was answered when I was seated. I sat with my head in my hands and began to cry and as I cried, God spoke through somebody in tongues. It was so beautiful; I knew it was you God and that you hurt too; you were crying with us.

I felt a release within me and a peace filled me. I felt hands upon me. I was really crying. One or two people interpreted the tongues but then someone else said quite strongly, "My dearest children"…but I clearly heard "My Dear Child," which was the title of a book given to me on our baptism day; and then they spoke of 'Your love pouring out upon us Lord' and it was wonderful, and it was real. Thank you. Last out again and sleeping tablets for James and I when we got home and that was another day done.

Monday 2nd February 2004

Things to organise! Alan was brilliant. It was a good, positive and very powerful day – God's hand was upon every detail, clearing the way for Friday's services.

The school put out a book of condolences for the kids to write in and Philip and the church care team and other church leaders from Chipping Campden and Moreton were there. The Headmaster spoke about Tom and then Philip spoke and prayed. They had a time of silence for Tom, then the majority of Yr 11's left and there was a core group of about forty. They split into small groups and talked and cried with the guys from church. It was a good time and the right people were there for them. Alan and I had woken up feeling that we really wanted to be there with them but we knew that it was right that we weren't.

Daniel came and took James to Cleeve Hill, something James felt drawn to doing, and we went to Shipston 'tip' (life goes on!) and then on to the Riverside Christian Centre: a retreat centre run by two 'mature' ladies. We hadn't planned to go and had never been before, although we knew people who helped out in the coffee room and shop, but we wanted a couple of cards so we went. We were wonderfully looked after by two friends, who insisted on feeding us and while we were eating a song came on the C.D. player that we felt was perfect for the service on Friday morning but it wasn't a song that we had ever heard before. It was *O let the son of God enfold you,* an old song, but the words and tune just spoke volumes of how we were being held close by Jesus. If I heard it now I'd be a weeping wreck!

Then we went to Banbury to pick up Alan's sister, Liz, from the bus station as she wanted to come and stay and support us. Once we were home we had another stream of visitors, some we knew were coming and some we didn't. I think we only had time to put the kettle on before the first ones came! Mums from school and neighbours all came and cried in our kitchen. Sharon and Dave – a young couple from church had offered to bring a meal. I remember feeling very strongly that I wanted them there but didn't really know why. Sharon was great. She just took over the kitchen! More friends came– it was after six by now. Phil called in for a cuppa and then left and we just spent time talking about events since Friday. It was good for Liz to be part of it and she could see where we were at.

Eventually all the visitors left and we thought we could eat, but there was a knock at the door and when I opened it there was a sea of faces – all Year 10's and Tom's friends. We welcomed them in and sat with them in the lounge. Alan sat on the floor and we just chatted about Tom and his faith. It was a special time! They were Moreton kids who knew Tom from the school bus and the gigs. Matt put a card through the door and so we called him in too; it was good and a real witness of God's love.

I had a really good chat on the phone with Mum about where she stood in her faith and about Alpha. Why did Tom have to die before I got the courage to ask? We'd meant to for months… (Please God continue to give me the words and the courage to speak when I meet people and give me opportunities to speak). She said Dad was not so strong and could not believe in a God of love who would let Tom do what he did so would rather believe in no God at all.

Eventually we ate (must have been about 9pm)!! After dinner we all felt we should pray. As Dave was praying, I thought about 'the valley of the shadow of death' we were walking through and felt we weren't walking through it but being carried above it.

Alan began to speak out my thoughts in his prayers, at the same time, and God gave me a strong picture of each time we sank into the valley we were being lifted on eagle's wings, (as a mother eagle will swoop down and lift her young if they're not ready to fly and be carried on the eagle's wings above the valley again). Such peace! Only through God's love and the prayers of so many people had we come through thus far.

Tuesday 3rd February 2004

A quiet morning, I think; made ourselves eat toast for breakfast – for Liz's sake really. Had a phone call from school, 'I've got four lads here who want to come over. Can I bring them?"

"Yes of course," we said; no hesitation! So we waited for them to arrive, talking over last night and the events since Friday and started to open some of the twenty cards that came that morning.

I am sorry I can't remember exactly who came – lads that hadn't been before. Anyway they were so welcome and so brave. Whoever brought them stayed out in the car and we just chatted about Tom and school, and of course Tom's faith. Then they were taken back to school.

We all felt we needed some air, so we walked down into Moreton and picked up rolls and doughnuts for lunch from the shop where I worked. We met David Bryant – a lovely gentleman from church who is so gifted at flower arranging. He said the Tuesday market flower man was ill and not on his stall and David was not sure what he was going to do about flowers for the church for Friday's Thanksgiving service for Tom. Well, we had bucket-loads at home, with no vases or space to put them, so we offered them to David – another example of God's hand in the situation. It was lovely to know, on Friday, that the flowers in church had been given to us in love and we were able to pass them on with the same love so that more people would see them and benefit from them. David did a great job and the church looked beautiful.

A friend drove Liz home, back to Hitchin. I'm not sure that we spent that much time with her as so much else was going on – but it was good that she came. Alan and I went to Cheltenham to see the Coroners' officer. I think James had gone into school to spend some time with his old Head of Year and others who knew him.

The Coroners' officer was very nice and the visit was not as bad as we'd feared. It made the whole thing horribly real in a nitty-gritty way but had to be done. He talked us through every step, for that visit and visits to come, told us that the cause of death on the certificate had to be hanging – well it was true – but it was good to be warned, and helped us later in the week when the papers came out.

Afterwards we went round the corner to the tearoom where James worked for a fortifying cup of tea (and a much needed sugar boost!). It helped us to get through the coroners' visit to know that that haven was only a short walk away, just another touch of God's hand on the situation.

After Monday, Tuesday felt like a really bad day and I felt quite low – we'd woken up feeling that way and it didn't really get any better. We had just put on a brave face for Liz. We were home from Cheltenham quite late – after 5pm. We had spoken to James as he was leaving the school in Campden and he was happy to be home first and do the dogs so imagine my fears when we arrived home and his car was not in the drive! We rang Helen, in case he had popped round there, quite understandable if he'd been unable to go into the empty house (it was becoming a stumbling block for me) but he wasn't there. My poor little heart was beating so fast and I felt sick as I didn't know where he was, –imagining all sorts of things – and fearing I'd lost him too. But he'd called into the teashop, I worked in, and stayed chatting!

I guess those fears are something I am going to have to work really hard at and trust God for James when he is out.

In the evening Philip and the Friday music group called round. I don't know if they'd all planned to come together or if it just worked that way but it was good to begin planning Friday's services, again – more reality and decisions but with great support. We felt really blessed that the organ in the crematorium was broken and so we were able to have our own musicians. We have nothing against organs or organists but for us it made it extra special.

James went to a youth group, taken there by two girls, and bought home by another. Everyone has been there for him too, whatever and whenever we've needed. God has sent provision – awesome!

Wednesday 4th February 2004

Woke up before 7:00am with the words for my piece on Friday; came downstairs and wrote them on a piece of paper. Felt very sad. Went back to bed for a cry and a cuddle but knew they were exactly the right words for me and I had no need to change them. Felt peace again.

Once we were up Wednesday turned into a really bad day! We had to be at the undertakers in Brailes at 10:00am so arranged to pick Philip up on route and to leave the key out for Mum, Dad and my sister who were coming to do lunch and sort out all the flowers in the house (not my strong point at all, I really am hopeless with flowers!). Anyway we were halfway to Brailes when I suddenly realised I had forgotten to leave the key and so no one could get in and they'd have to sit on the doorstep until we got back. I rang Dad and explained and they came and waited in the teashop where I worked – a good time for them, I think.

Again we were not looking forward to the undertakers but God was with us and carried us through. James has been involved in every decision at every stage and it's been the three of us, all the way. It was good to have Phil there. He was so matter of fact and a source of calm. He helped with decisions about flowers and cars and following the coffin (or not), a decision we put off until Thursday. I remember not knowing what Tom should wear in his coffin and feeling quite unnerved by it – and should I send underwear and what about shoes…we settled on the clothes that he, himself, had recently bought as it seemed right, but I don't remember about underwear or shoes. I may have sent them but whether he was dressed in them I don't know.

The inquest was opened and adjourned and so we then had to deal with the press. We had already had the guy from the Cotswold Journal; we had told him that we would print something and give to him the next day. We gave him a school photo of Tom and a press release which we gave to everyone telling of Tom's love for others, his faith and our love for him. So, that was what we gave each paper and if they wanted more (which they did) they didn't get it.

After lunch, Alan went to The Riverside Centre, to make arrangements for Friday, when our families would go over for a light lunch after the crematorium service and before the Thanksgiving – Phil's suggestion and a very good one. I stayed home with everyone else and went through a shaky time. I had to deal with a woman reporter and virtually had to throw her out of the house; I only let her in because we had to print off some more press releases and it would have been rude to leave her on the doorstep with the door closed.

James was on the computer looking for Tom's baptism testimony, which Philip wanted to use on Friday in the Thanksgiving service. We found a file that Tom had written two weeks before. It was hard to cope with as it was a potted history of how he'd felt since he was seven but so powerfully and beautifully written – such a waste of talent – but too much talent perhaps? The hardest part was realising he'd only written it a short time before. Why couldn't he tell someone who could help?

Alan came home and we told him about the file. He had found it the night before and felt it wasn't the right time to show it to us, but hey, at least we all know now.

Tom's friends came round with the song that they had composed and put on to a C.D. for Tom. We listened to it with tears in our eyes; it was beautiful and very Tom. They stayed for about half an hour and again we just chatted. It was a good time.

Friends, Andy and Angela came for tea – sorry guys it wasn't up to much! James went to Stratford and out for a meal with a couple of girlfriends and we went to the church meeting. Andy drove us in their car and we arrived just in time for Andy to lead worship (in other words – late!) which was a really good time. It was good to stand together, and be real, and show our emotions – and good because the Lord ministered to us again, filled us up and enabled us to cope. Again, where else would we go?

James came home at 11:45pm and Andy and Angela were still there. There was so much peace in our house, no one wanted to go home! I suspect though that Andy and Ange just wanted to be sure James got home safely. Thanks guys – you're special!

Thursday 5th February 2004

Woke up feeling it was a good day. We'd had no post on Wednesday, which was odd, and at 9:00am we had forty one cards come streaming through the letterbox. It was so funny, like the scene from Harry Potter and so very Tom. He would have loved it, although I did apologise to the postman the next day, for my hysterical laughter, as the cards just kept on coming!

We had arranged to meet Mum at Wellesbourne Crematorium at 10:00am, a really good idea of James's as he had never been to one before. Alan had never been there and Mum hadn't been since her parents' ashes had been scattered there many years before. It was a good time for her. We were able to go into the North Chapel and decide where we wanted to sit etc. It was very peaceful.

We met Philip for lunch and then planned the services with him, what in which order etc, and went down to organise the church. We put out a hundred and seventy chairs (not physically ourselves, they were there already, in case any one reading this really does think we're superhuman!) and there was room for fifty on the balcony, so two hundred and twenty places altogether.

James put all the songs and Tom's photo on to PowerPoint and we played the kids' song so that we knew it would work okay. David's flowers were lovely! The arrangement seemed to me to be a hand reaching up – and we know God's hands were reaching down; again, it was good to know that flowers given to us had been used to decorate the church.

Then we prayed together because we had to go to Brailes to see Tom's body – another thing we were dreading doing. We met Mum and Dad over there and had decided that we'd all go in together. Then we would leave Mum and Dad with Tom for a while and then we'd go in and say our goodbyes. Well, we all went in together, took one look, said, "That's not Tom." (It was of course!) and promptly relaxed. James said it was just a shell. Tom would have died of embarrassment at what they'd done to his hair –fluffy and with a centre parting! Mum felt that we'd all said goodbye on Friday evening in his room and that the Sunday morning service was when everyone else did.

Back to Mum and Dad's for a cup of tea, then home, and more kids or visitors. Someone bought a lovely tea and pudding to fortify us for the day ahead, which was a blessing.

Alan put together a service sheet for the morning with Bible verses top and bottom. Alan chose the top one: *"Be still and know that I am God; I will be exalted among the nations, I will be exalted in the earth"* (Psalm 46v10). And I chose: *"Live a life filled with love for others, following the example of Christ, who loved you and gave himself as a sacrifice to take away your sins"* (Ephesians 5v2) (because that's what Tom's life was –filled with love for others) and at the bottom of the sheet we put, *"Love you always Tom. See you later!"*

While Alan did that I wrote the last verse to the poem I was going to read, just to personalise it to Tom – "Oh Father, you have called him, your precious child of grace, help us Lord look up to you, 'till we all meet face to face'." Then at about 1:00am we went to bed!

Friday 6th February 2004
Tom's Cremation and Thanksgiving Services

An awesome day! Where do I start? I suppose, when we got up – early. Alan went to church to photocopy the service sheets and to give them to Philip. James and I did the usual morning things – letting the dogs out, tidying up, etc. Alan came home and cooked us all a 'Tom' breakfast – sausage, bacon and croissants. Helen came round to pray. Alan washed the car – missed more than he washed! We showered and changed and then drove to The Riverside Christian Centre.

We'd arranged to meet Mum, Dad and Daniel there. Daniel was chauffeur for Mum and Dad as we felt Mum shouldn't drive, (Dad was unable to drive anymore due to eyesight problems). We three felt okay about going in our own car – it felt right. Once everyone had arrived, we set off to Wellesbourne, a quiet and contemplative journey, none of us knowing how to feel.

Arrived, lots of cars and people – I suppose about forty altogether, lots of hugging and tears. We went in to the North Chapel and prayed with Phil, Hermey and the music group, and then we just waited for Tom to arrive. When all was ready they took the coffin inside and put the flowers on the table. We walked in, as a family, with friends behind while the musicians played 'I want to be out of my depth in your love' because that's how we've felt all week.

Philip welcomed everyone and we stayed seated for *Be still for the presence of the Lord*. I can't remember much of what Phil said next – (sorry Phil!) except that he said he felt too far away from us, because of the layout of the chapel. He read a story about a ship leaving and disappearing from view, only to be seen appearing on the horizon (it was lovely but Alan and I can't remember it all now). We stood for *Great is the Lord* and felt His love and presence as we worshipped Him. Then it was the committal and the curtains closed around the coffin. I remember I wanted to run to the coffin, tear off the lid, pick Tom up and take him home – but I stayed glued to my seat – as you do.

We stayed seated for *O let the Son of God enfold you* which was the song we'd heard at The Riverside Christian Centre on Monday. It was beautiful and peaceful and healing – you could just feel God's love as we sang. Then we left the building and the undertaker met us at the door; he said he had been touched by the service.

We then had to say goodbye to everyone, one by one in a long file past the awful flowers – we had asked for an arrangement of the letters **TOM** to be white chrysanths with a yellow centre, (you know the sort of thing), but they came bright orange with a yellow centre and clashed terribly. Nothing we could do, and in the scheme of things it shouldn't have mattered, but it did. They were hideous! I was doing okay until I saw Tom's best friend, from junior school, who we hadn't seen since his family moved away five or six years before. We made eye contact and I recognised him immediately. Our hearts just seemed to go out to each other – he had been so nervous of meeting us and not knowing what to say; and they'd arrived late so he hadn't seen us before the service but we just hugged and cried. It was a lovely moment; I am so pleased he and his mum came.

Eventually everyone had gone and we drove back to The Riverside where the families were meeting for lunch – the ladies had done us proud. The table looked lovely: quiche, sandwiches, crisps etc and tea and coffee. I remember feeling it was all a bit surreal, people making 'normal' conversations and asking us about the history of The Centre. I really struggled to cope and just wanted to go. We left just after 2pm and made our way to Campden for the Thanksgiving Service.

The Ship

"From "Westminster sermons," by W.E. Sangster

'Some time ago, an army officer (it was Colonel David Marcus) was killed in action. Before he was buried, the contents of his pockets were put together and sent to his widow.

She was greatly comforted by one thing that he was carrying when he died. No, it wasn't a letter addressed to her; it was a little bit of paper entitled, "The Ship." We don't know where he got it from. We only know how much it meant to her.

"I am standing upon the sea shore. A ship at my side spreads white sails to the morning breeze and starts for the blue ocean. She is an object of beauty and strength, and I stand and watch her until, at length she is only a ribbon of white cloud just where the sea and sky come to mingle with each other. Then someone at my side says, "There, she's gone."

Gone where? Gone from my sight that is all. She is just as large in mast and hull and spar as she was when she left my side and just as able to bear her load of living freight to the place of destination. Her diminished size is in me, not in her, and just at that moment when someone at my side says, "There, she's gone" there are other voices ready to take up the glad shout, "There she comes."

And that is dying for the Christian.'

Tom's Thanksgiving Service 3:00pm

Chipping Campden Baptist Church

We arrived at about 2:15pm and the church was already quite full. As we drove down the High Street we passed the school-friends (the school had allowed fifty to attend the service but many more had wanted to come) walking through Campden on their way to church, and our hearts went out to them – some of them saw us and waved. I think we waved back – can't remember!

Once in the church we felt like we were 'on show' as people seemed to be watching us (probably because we weren't weeping and wailing but walking around greeting people). We said, "Hi," to some of Tom's friends, the ones who'd come to the house. (We had taken a few moments to get changed and they had come in and sat down by the time we went into the church itself).

At about 2:40pm we couldn't take anymore of the 'goldfish' feeling so we went upstairs to pray with Phil and the worship group – which is what we wanted to do - and then sat for ten minutes until the service started at 3:00pm. It was lovely because the worship group played and sang (Thanks guys, you were all brill!) and those in the congregation that knew the words sang quietly. It was really peaceful and a lovely way to start the service.

Philip welcomed everyone and then we all stood and sang, *Be thou my Vision*. I remember, into the third verse, my sister broke down. It was good to be able to go to her and hold her (and keep singing such powerful words over her). Then we sang *Shine Jesus Shine*. The words were so real – *Lord the light of your love is shining*…We had chosen to include this song because Alan hated it. Tom knew that and bizarrely we thought he might be watching the service and find it funny! But actually the words are really good, as I've said.

The reading was from Isaiah 40v25-31, *To whom will you compare me? Or who is my equal?" says the Holy One. Lift your eyes and look to the heavens: Who created all of these? He who brings out the starry host one by one, and calls them each by name. Because of His great power and mighty strength, not one of them is missing. Why do you say, O Jacob, and complain, O Israel, "My way is hidden*

27

from the Lord; my cause is disregarded by my God"? Do you not know? Have you not heard? The LORD is the everlasting God, the Creator of the ends of the earth. He will not grow tired or weary, and His understanding no one can fathom. He gives strength to the weary and increases the power of the weak. Even youths grow tired and weary, and young men stumble and fall; but those who hope in the LORD will renew their strength. They will soar on wings like eagles; they will run and not grow weary, they will walk and not be faint.

Then it was my turn. I read the bit I had prepared and the poem *God Lent a Child* with the last verse I had added on. I thought I was going to pass out before I got up to speak but the Lord held me and made me strong and clear when I spoke. We sang, *The Lord's my Shepherd* (the modern version, which was beautiful.) It was funny though because there was a problem with the computer and getting the words on to the screen, so James had to go and help!

Then we played the song that Tom's friends had written, which was lovely, and lots of tissues were needed, but it was great for the school friends to feel they had done their part. Alan spoke next – he was amazing, so relatable and relaxed, God's hands supporting him too. He read Tom's writing 'The Walk' first and then Tom's Baptism Testimony, complete and unaltered, even to the bit where Tom had looked around the church for Stevie T (his Junior school teacher, who ran a Christian club called Pathfinders, at the school and who most likely introduced Tom to Jesus, but I don't know that for certain) and thanked him for coming all the way from Derbyshire. It was bizarre to see Alan do the same and for Steve to be sitting in the same block of seats.

We sang *My Jesus, My Saviour* (Tom and Alan's baptism song) and the headmaster led a tribute time. Several people came forward to speak, also quite a few of Tom's close friends. It was good to see them get up and speak to a packed church with such confidence, I think – a measure of how highly they thought of Tom.

Daniel led prayers and then Philip spoke the message – exactly what people needed to hear. When something like this happens we want answers, to know why, because then we can deal with it, keep it neat and tidy, put it in a box and it goes away. But there are only two people who know why – Tom and God, so we have to wait and trust.

Philip said, "Answers are not always the last word. We live in a hard cynical world that would love to have an easy answer, that would love to wrap it up, label it and say 'that's done with' but there are no easy answers. Reasons and answers today are not our deepest need; our deepest need today is God. We don't have the answers but our comfort and strength is that God does. Trust the man who lived and died and rose again – Jesus – as Tom did. Believe the Bible that says 'For God so loved the world that he gave His one and only Son that whoever believes in Him will not perish but have eternal life. The most important decision Tom ever made was to accept Jesus for himself. I believe Tom is more alive now than he ever was, he is more at peace now than he ever was."

Then we sang the last two songs – *No Eye has Seen* and *There is a Day,* a strong and powerful ending!

Alan and I jumped up and went to the door; to be there for all the school kids as they went out and an hour and a half later we were still there! I felt guilty for those who felt they had to give us a hug. I wish they'd just shaken hands or something but there were those who needed to be hugged as they left – I remember one lady; she hugged me for <u>me</u>; it was a blessing to receive that hug and we needed no words.

Don't know how many were in the church for the service – I know many were standing but it was so good to praise the Lord and give Him glory for Tom's life; many people were touched by it.

So, of course, we were last out again, tired but full of the Lord's goodness. At just after 9pm, Philip, Daniel and Helen came around to take communion with us. Hermey had baked us a tiny loaf, just right for six! It was a special time and a fitting end to the day.

<u>Saturday 7<u>th</u> February 2004</u>

An empty day – picked things up – and put them down again; that sort of day!

We tidied up a bit, in Tom's room, as I wanted to wash his and James's sheets etc. Found the diary behind his bed that he had mentioned in his letter to us (the police had missed it). It made hard reading – I looked at it emotionally, (language, drinking, other things he'd done, things he'd thought etc – but, hey, he was growing up) and Alan read it logically and bought me back to the facts.

Nowhere in it did it say that he didn't believe in God anymore; you could tell that he did but that he was doing things <u>his</u> (Tom's) way. It helped us to understand a bit more where he was coming from and what he was going through.

We had been offered the use of a house in Kingsbridge, Devon, by some friends of Bev and Paul – it's amazing how people wanted to help and support us even though we did not know them. We didn't want to go, but everyone said it would be a good idea, so we picked up the keys at 5pm when the shop was closed. It was good to talk through the service with them; they have been a tremendous support to us all.

Alan played his guitar and I read my Bible, and for the first time it became a living word – I underlined things and dated them February 2004. Psalm 34 really spoke to me and comforted me, especially the last verse. (No I am not going to print it – you'll have to look it up yourself!!!) It was a good and positive end to the day.

Sunday 8<u>th</u> February 2004

This needed to be a 'closure' service for the church, so we could all move on and people needed to know that what Tom did was wrong. He <u>is</u> with the Lord but it is not the right way to get there; it is not a good short cut to heaven. We stood and thanked the church for their love, prayers and support. I shared my picture of being carried on eagle's wings and James thanked the students that had been such a support to him.

Philip preached from Psalm 42 and spoke of God being our Rock in times of desperation and even though the Psalmist is desolate and cannot see God, he still says, *I will put my hope in God! I will praise Him again – my Saviour and my God!* (Just as Alan and I have done. To whom else would we run?)

Afterwards we went outside with the junior church children and said a prayer, and Philip told them Tom had gone to be with Jesus, and we let three balloons go. (It was supposed to be thirty but James ran out of helium after three, which we felt was quite appropriate and we know Tom would have seen the funny side too!).

A lady shared with us a picture she had had on Friday, of Lazarus and the way Jesus had allowed him to suffer and die, in order to bring glory to God's name and how she felt God would use this whole thing powerfully.

I felt that God was preparing us as a church family, drawing us closer to Him, to our knees and preparing us for His purposes. We must each allow Him to work in us and through us, to submit totally to His will, even when it hurts, and to praise Him <u>always</u> and for <u>everything</u>.

Then we went down to Devon, to a cottage lent to us by Christians that we didn't know but given in Christian love. I felt very strongly that I should write down all that had happened in the last week, which is what you are reading now – some bits have been added to 'make more sense' and also as I have remembered more. I am not a writer – nor do I want to become one but I felt I had to capture everything that we'd felt and experienced so that's what I spent the time doing. We only managed to stay for two nights and by Tuesday we just had to get home – couldn't stand being away any longer – although it was a beautiful and peaceful place.

Throughout this whole awful time – from finding Tom, to his services the following week – we have learnt how real our God is. He has truly moved from our heads to our hearts. We are so thankful to Him for the deep sense of peace we've felt in our hearts and throughout the house. We've truly been upheld in God's love and grace, through the prayers and actions of God's people from Cornerstone churches and beyond.

Paths have been smoothed before us. Things that could have been really hard have been surprisingly easy. We've wept tears of love – for Tom – because we sort of understand, through his letters and writings, why he couldn't face the future and for ourselves, because we have to face a future without him. But even through the tears, we have the absolute conviction that we <u>will</u> see Tom again and when we do, we can hold him and hug him and say to him – "I do, now, understand you."

The Lord will redeem those who serve Him. Everyone who trusts in Him will be freely pardoned. (Psalm 34v22).

Hindsight can be a wonderful thing. We can see that writing was Tom's way of reaching out, especially in the last twelve months but he always said he didn't know where it came from – we only saw the brilliance of the writing. He couldn't open his heart to us to show us his pain – was that to save us hurt in his big-hearted generous way? Tom's writing <u>was</u> a gift from God. Even in his darkest times that brilliance has helped us to cope and to understand, when maybe we wouldn't have without it.

So what now? – A future of hope and promise of eternal life awaits us but until then we must seek the Lord's will and what He would have us do with all that we've experienced. We've learnt that all things work to the good for those who trust Him and that His timing is perfect and that He will use all things to bring glory to his name; all we have to do is trust him!

Saturday 14th February 2004

Well, we thought we were doing okay, getting back to some sort of normality, and getting ready to go back to work etc, when along comes Satan and kicks us right where it hurts.

We received some information that just left us reeling – empty and hopeless but it was nothing to do with Tom directly. We spent about twenty four hours building this thing into a huge, mental monster and sinking deeper into despair.

We knew it was something we had to face head on as we've faced so many things that way over the last couple of weeks. So, we looked to the Lord, took our eyes off ourselves, dealt with the information and showed Satan the door. The peace is back in our hearts and we know we can cope again. Thank you Lord, another lesson learnt.

We learnt – it matters not how – that Tom's best friend knew what Tom was going to do because Tom had shared it with him one time when he came to stay. He had shown him what he was going to use and do.

The shock of knowing that was enormous. Why didn't his friend say something – to anyone – to us? If only he had, Tom might still be here. But then, how could he? He was fifteen and maybe he thought Tom was messing about and wouldn't go through with it.

Our hearts went out to him (and still do – he has to live with that knowledge for all his life) and we realised that we had to forgive him and love him and move on.

He doesn't know that we know. Maybe one day we'll get to talk with him – I feel that he needs to know that we know and that we don't blame him for not saying.

If I were to write an epitaph for Tom, it would come out of what we've discovered from something he wrote in January and it would be, "Tom was everything to everyone that they needed or wanted him to be except to himself; such was his generosity."

Thanks Tom. We love you!!

Empty Hearts and Empty Praises

Empty hearts and empty praises,
Do not let them be,
Restore us and renew us Lord
As we look up to Thee.

We want to see revival Lord,
Our hearts cry out to You.
We know there's so much hurt and pain
And a mighty work to do.

So Father lift and teach us, in your gentle way,
In each experience to seek
Your heavenly face, your lessons Lord,
Your strength when we are weak.

Let not these weeks be wasted,
Nor Tom's life be gone in vain,
His love for You was awesome Lord,
Help ours to be the same.

To stand for You and fight for You
When the going seems quite tough,
To lift our hearts, cry out to You –
Even praise, when it's not enough.

When my soul cries out in wanting 'more'
And 'more' just won't suffice,
That's when I need to listen Lord
And heed your quiet advice.

So speak to each as You know how,
Through prayer and song and word,
Tell us Lord Your plans for us,
And let us know that You have heard.

When we give our hearts to you afresh
Our very lives for You,
Our every breath, our every deed.
Know every promise Lord is true.

Jackie. 22. February 2004

34

Tom

I'm overwhelmed with love for you
I'm sorry it's too late,
Why couldn't I tell you more –?
I love you, thank you, you're great!

Why did you have to die before
These feelings came to me?
I took you so much for granted,
Your qualities I just couldn't see.

I was so busy with my own life,
With work and church and stuff,
I did not realise when you were down
Or talk to you nearly enough.

Perhaps if I had, you'd still be here
With your quiet smile and charm,
You touched so many people Tom
And we've had so much to learn.

Your death has taught us many things –
About love and faith and fear,
About ourselves and how you felt
And about our God who's always near.

He took your hand and took you home
To where you knew was love,
I'm sorry Tom we didn't show you here
As much care as He did above.

So Tom I just want to say,
I love you, I'm so proud of you,
I'm glad your pain has gone,
Forgive me when I cry for you – my precious, lovely son.

Jackie. 23. February 2004

What Will it Take?

What will it take till we're on our knees
Crying out to You, our King?
Until You see our hearts are pure
And we mean what we pray and sing.

We need to learn to fear You Lord
To come in reverent praise.
To worship at Your throne of Grace
And marvel at Your ways.

To seek forgiveness of our sins
With truly humble hearts,
We don't deserve Your love and Grace
Your mercy or what it imparts.

We pray to You and You bless our lives
And we think that's all there is,
But Jesus <u>died</u> so we'd be free –
Gave <u>His</u> life that we might live.

We've made You far too cosy Lord
We've made You what <u>we</u> want,
Its time to wake us from our sleep –
To lead us from the front.

And if the lessons are hard or hurt
So may Your will be done,
Teach us any way You can
To see your Kingdom come.

Renew in us a passion Lord,
Revive our hearts we pray
Stir us into action now
Till on our knees we'll stay.

We'll pray to You and cry out Your name
From the depths of our very souls
We'll call upon Your awesome power
Until your mercy freely falls.

When Your heart is filled with love for us
And You know that we truly repent,
We'll seek Your will for each of us
And give our lives in obedience.

Then You'll see us on our knees –
Our tears will freely flow.
We'll rise as one with one accord
And in Your name we'll go.

Jackie. 24. February 2004

God's Love

In times of quiet reflection
As I think upon your ways.
My heart is filled with amazing love
And I'm lost in awe and praise.

When I gaze into the moonlit night
 See the stars so crystal clear,
I think upon your majesty –
And your words fall in my ear;

"He gave His life for you my child,
He came to set you free,
So all your sins would be forgiven
And you'd come back to me.

To know the love I have for you –
Let nothing else suffice,
I formed you in the darkest place
And breathed you into life.

I know the plans I have for you,
The paths that you must tread,
I know the things that will hinder you
As you walk your ways instead.

And all the time I'll wait in love –
I'll watch from close by your side,
And when you're ready to come look for me,
My arms will be open wide.

I'll lead you if you'll take my hand,
I'll dry your tears with love,
I'll teach you what I want from you,
I'll show you heaven above".

Oh loving Father, how can this be?
That you would love us so,
We don't deserve your awesome grace –
But there's nowhere else to go.

To whom else can we run to?
When all we feel is pain,
When the hurt is just too much to bear
And we know life won't be the same.

But Father, you are constant
In a world that's full of change,
Thank you Lord for your great love,
You are always within our range.

Jackie. 25. February 2004

Why?

I stand in your room and I wonder why,
What thoughts were in your head?
And why you couldn't tell us,
So you took your life instead.

I stand in your room and I wonder how,
How you could feel so low
That you would take the bravest step,
I guess we'll never know.

I stand in your room and I wonder when
Those thoughts began to come,
It hurts, but I do understand
Why you couldn't tell me, your Mum.

I stand in your room and I wonder how
I could have been so blind,
So wrapped up I'm my cosy world
I never saw the signs.

I stand in your room and I wonder why
You couldn't reach out to me,
You kept it all inside your mind,
There was nothing for us to see.

I stand in your room and I wonder when
You sank deeper into despair,
We all loved you so very much
But you thought that we didn't care.

I stand in your room and I wonder why,
It all seems such a waste,
You gave so much to everyone
You will never be replaced.

I stand in your room and I know why
You did what you had to do,
You knew with every ache in your heart
Our God was waiting for you.

I stand in your room and I feel such peace,
I know you are in heaven above,
God took your hand when you needed him most
And enfolded you in His love.

I stand in your room and I wonder how
Your memory will live on,
It will live in the hearts of all those you have touched,
You were one in a million, Tom.

Jackie 4. March 2004

Turn the Clock Back

I want to turn the clock back,
I'd give anything to be able to.
I just want one more chance
To stand and look up at you.

To stand with my head on your shoulder,
The way you'd look down at me,
I was so proud to be your mum –
You were all I could hope you could be.

I wish I had just one more day,
To tell you things I should have said,
So that you'd know you were loved
And not listened to words in your head.

Your future was so hopeful,
There was so much you could have done….
You could have changed the world Tom,
Now all hope, it seems is gone.

I'd give my life to have you back,
But what would that achieve?
I must learn to carry on – for other's sake,
In giving will I receive?

Forgive my crying aching heart,
I'm just your poor old Mum,
I know you told me not to,
But this crying's not for fun.

It's just I really want you back,
The way things used to be,
That we would be a family of four
Instead of a grieving three.

So there you go, I've poured it out,
I've told you how I feel,
I feel a little better now —
I just wish it wasn't so real.

Jackie. 6. March 2004

Good Times?

There must have been times in your life Tom,
When everything was going just great,
You had so much to look forward to –
Why did your heart have to break?

We had some fun as a family,
It wasn't all work and no play.
There were times of great joy and rejoicing,
Why did pain have to get in the way?

I know there were times when we shouted
And times when you felt out of place,
But mostly there were times of companionship,
Did you think it all such a waste?

Sometimes it was 'let's get at Tom day'
That's how it seemed to me,
But that was only a part of growing up –
Why did you not let us see

How much you were hurting inside Tom,
The scars that cut so deep,
That you couldn't bear to tell us
The secrets you tried to keep?

I know you knew you were loved Tom,
And I guess that's why you tried
To cope with it all in your own way,
By keeping it bottled inside.

You didn't want to hurt us,
And for that we're truly blessed,
You only wanted to hurt yourself,
Not give heartache to all the rest.

You couldn't see a way out Tom,
Except to heaven above,
And now you're in peace for eternity
Safe in God's arms of love.

Jackie. 7. March 2004

James

You are my firstborn precious son,
You mean the world to me.
You've been the one I talk to,
The one whose let me 'be'

You've listened to my troubles
Whilst to and fro into town,
In all your years of growing up
You've never let me down.

You were the one to whom
The toughest standards I set.
But throughout all your childhood
Those standards you always met.

And now you're growing older,
Your whole life ahead of you,
You're a son to be rightly proud of,
(you're pretty good looking too!)

You've had to deal with the toughest thing,
No brother should have to face,
And through it all, though it's been hard,
You've kept your smile in place.

So I pray God's hand upon your life,
His richest blessings for you,
That you would know you are truly loved
As our son (and Tom's brother too)

Jackie. 8. March 2004

More Than Words

I want to give You more than words,
Lord, I give my life to You,
 That I would open up my heart
And let Your love shine through.
The hope I have, I know is real,
It's in my heart, not just my head.
Help me now draw near to You
And by Your Holy Spirit be led.

And as I walk through darkest days,
I know You're right beside me,
Your loving arms are open wide
To lead me and to guide me.
Jesus, you gave your life for me,
A sacrifice upon the cross,
For all my sins to be forgiven
You paid the highest cost.

Teach me Lord, as I walk with You,
Give me courage and words to say,
That through Your love and healing power,
People will know of You today.
Renew in me a passion Lord,
 A hunger for Your name,
So I would truly stand for You
And lead others to do the same.

This crazy world is all but lost,
the devil thinks he's won,
But we have power and victory's shout
Through Jesus Christ, Your Son.
Oh, Lord our time is running out,
We need to win this race,
So many souls still left to save,
So many who need your grace.

Equip us and protect us Lord
As we seek to spread Your word,
Lead us now according to Your will
To those who haven't heard.
We bow our heads before You now,
Lift our hands to Your heavenly Throne,
Help us reap a mighty harvest Lord,
So You can call the lost Your own.

Jackie. 10. March 2004

I wrote this poem after we had been to the cinema to see The Passion of The Christ on its release. I found myself watching Mary throughout – maybe because of the mother bond; anyway that is why I felt led to write this.

Mary

Mary, I share your sorrow, you too have lost a son,
Though very different circumstances, we share our grief as one.
Mary, you were chosen, to bear God's only child,
You nursed him and took care of Him, our Saviour, meek and mild.

I wonder when you understood, how special He would be,
And how you had to let Him go, so He could set us free.
How terrible it must have been, to watch Him suffer so,
You must have really felt His pain, and in His place longed to go.

How precious was that moment, when you held Him in your arms,
Even though His life was gone, God's love helped you stay calm.
I've shared that peace from God above; I've known just how you felt,
When I kissed my Tom goodbye that night, as by his side I knelt.

I too was chosen, God entrusted Tom to me,
To love him and take care of him, help him be all that he could be.
And though Tom took his own life, he knew of Jesus' love,
He knew through all his hurt and pain, God was watching from above.

Our sons' have touched so many hearts, in so many different ways,
But now they're safe for eternity, and to God's name bring praise.
So Mary, though we've never met, we share each others pain,
But through our tears, we know this truth; our loss is heavens' gain.

Jackie. 27. March 2004

<u>J</u>esus

Why do I feel the way I feel
When my heart cries out to you?
Why do the tears begin to fall
When I know you love me too?

Why do I feel so humbled
When I think of all you've done?
You took away my guilt and shame
When you died, God's only Son.

When desperate in the garden
You cried to God above
"Take this cup away from me"
You showed such amazing love.

In obedience to your father
You said "Your will be done",
What lessons you have taught us
That's where <u>my</u> heart was won.

You took my sin upon that cross
You did it all for me
My debt to you is priceless –
You suffered to set me free

So I would come to know you
And learn of God's perfect grace
And know the promise of eternity
Meeting You face to face.

Until that time you have my life
To do with as you choose
To mould me, break me, make me whole
And in your love, renewed

That's why I feel the way I feel
When my heart cries out your name
My gratitude is so immense
My life cannot be the same

Jackie. 1. April 2004

I wrote this poem, as an answer to all those who feel they have a right or that they are qualified to judge what Tom did – they were not there, they do not know the circumstances, only Tom and God know, and we feel we understand. So, in reading this poem, please put yourself in the 'you' of the first five verses and then understand that we <u>know</u> exactly where God was – and still is – in this whole situation.

<u>Where Were You?</u>

Where were You on that Friday night,
In January 2004?
When our precious son ended his life,
Because he couldn't take anymore?

Where were You when he took the noose,
And put it around his neck?
When he fell into unconsciousness
And God, his Father, met?

Where were You in that desperate time,
In the race to save his life?
In the disbelief at what he'd done –
Yet, somehow not being surprised?

Where were You in that peace-filled room,
As we knelt and prayed for Tom?
When I gently kissed his forehead,
As only a mother can kiss her son?

Where were you as people came,
Making endless cups of tea?
Struggling to believe it at all,
United in our misery?

Lord, You were there that Friday night,
When Tom cried out to You
You took his hand and took him home,
And You were hurting too.

You were there through all the days
Of numbness, shock and grief.
You held us tight and drew us near,
You filled us with Your peace.

You know why this had to happen,
You knew what was in store for Tom,
You saved him from such torment,
We thank You that he's gone.

We know he's safe with You now,
We know we'll see him again,
Thank You for all that his life meant on earth,
Our great loss is heavens' gain.

Jackie. 2. April 2004

What If....

What if I died tomorrow
Will my life have been worthwhile?
Have I done all that I could have,
Have I gone the extra mile?

What will my life have stood for?
In all that I've said and done,
Have I made any impact?
How many hearts have I won?

What if I didn't have you Lord
To love me and make me complete?
Life wouldn't have any meaning –
I'd be just like the man on the street.

What if just one came to you Lord
Because of something I said,
Would all of heaven be rejoicing
As to your throne they were led?

What if we *each* told *one* person
Of Jesus' love for them,
And they, in turn, told another –
Is there room enough up in heaven?

I don't want to die tomorrow,
There's too much work to be done,
I want to see revival –
To see your kingdom come.

I want to stand for you Lord,
Be strong and brave and true,
To walk the paths you lead me
Until I'm called home to you.

Jackie. 9. April 2004

<u>Guilty?</u>

Moving on and moving forward,
Further away from that day,
Only the pain doesn't get any easier,
And you feel it again and again.
Time is supposed to heal us,
We're supposed to get on with our life,
We're supposed to put it behind us,
So why does it cut like a knife?

You think that you've overcome it,
But really it's just buried deep,
Why are you scared to let it all out –
To let go and have a good weep?
Is it the feelings of guilt that you hide?
Are you scared that you're really to blame?
There's truth in what he had written,
But you deny it all just the same.

That's what he said that you did,
Whenever he talked with you,
You didn't listen and you twisted things
So they fitted with your point of view.
You should have been more of a mother,
There was so much more you could have done,
Oh yes, you did all the basics,
But you just weren't 'there' for your son.

It hurts when you see all his school friends,
It hurts when you're faced with the truth —
That they have their lives all before them,
While your son died, cut from his youth,
You should have seen it coming,
You should have seen the signs,
They were there if only you'd looked,
Opened your eyes, not been so blind.

If you had taken more of an interest
In the things that he liked to do,
He might have felt that you cared then,
     might still be here for you.
It's no good wishing with all of your heart,
You could turn back the hands of time,
Put right all that was broken,
Before he reached the end of the line.

You've one more chance to put things right,
One day when we all meet again,
But until then, you'll carry on —
And learn to live with the pain.

Jackie. 30. April 2004

April, 12 weeks on...

I felt it was time to write about what has happened to us and how we've felt and coped in the last twelve weeks – it seems such a short time and yet also such a long time since Tom died. It is still hard to admit that he took his own life, committed suicide, killed himself, all those terms are somehow not how we want to express what happened. Even if they are the truth, in the same way, we still talk of his 'services' and not his funeral. It is still painful to tell people who do not know and to share the pain of those who have only recently found out for whatever reason and cannot believe that he has gone.

Alan took a month off work, which was all of February, and was able, through March, to use up his holiday from last year so that he only worked one or at most two days a week. This was a good healing time for him, although he kept himself busy. (Alan is not one for sitting around!). He dealt with all the practical and necessary things like letter writing and house cleaning and made sure we were all fed.

His birthday was on the 16th of February, a week after the services, and was a painful day. We wanted to celebrate it and yet also would have let it pass without recognition but we had decided months before (with Tom) that we would go to a local pub. So, we felt that it would be right to still go and we took Helen as an honorary fourth person! It was a good evening and we even managed to eat Banoffee Pancakes in honour of Tom!

Two days later we took James to Aberystwyth University for an open day. This was a difficult day, with so many emotions, most of which we tried to hide from James, as we knew this had to be a day where the focus was on him and his future. The 'Uni' had a good feel, laid back and relaxed but friendly and open too. We were given the usual talks in the lecture room and then taken around by two students. I found it really hard to be shown all the different places within the university that Tom would have enjoyed. It was hard to realise that it was something he was never going to do; and not be able to share any of those thoughts with Alan, for fear of James overhearing, although Alan was thinking along the same lines. I remember the tears on the way home when James was asleep in the back of the car.

Alan was seeing his doctor regularly – the same one who came out the night Tom died, which was good, but I struggled with seeing a doctor as it meant telling them about Tom and I couldn't do that. I was with another practice in Moreton and was disappointed that no-one had contacted me at all; it had been all over the local paper when all was said and done. I eventually went for an appointment with the nurse for my regular B12 injection. I was surprised that the nurse was unaware of what had happened but I felt quite proud of myself that I was able to talk to her about it. I thought I must have been 'on the mend' emotionally – how silly can you be!

On Friday 27th February, we buried Tom's ashes. It was a simple ceremony, at the top of the Manse garden. (Philip's suggestion, and the right place for Tom. He is buried with some amazing people who have had a real impact on the life of the Baptist church in Chipping Campden). There were only seven of us: we three, Mum and Dad, Helen and Phil.

Phil gave a reading; Alan read Psalm 46. Then Phil prayed and as Alan poured the ashes into the ground, I read a poem that I had written to Tom (entitled *Tom* and written on 23rd February). Phil prayed again; we stood for a few moments, hugged each other and then went for tea and solace in the manse. It was good and fitting and all felt right again. We had not known how we would feel or cope but although it was emotional and there were tears, it was gentle and God held us throughout.

During this time, I had returned to work. I went for a few hours to cover lunch in the week preceding the 14th February. I thought I'd had enough time off and was okay to go back and so I went full time the week after we went to Aberystwyth. Bev and Paul throughout were fantastic and gave me all the help, space and encouragement I needed.

The customers were all pleased to see me back and I felt okay. In the bad moments I could go home if I needed to or I could work it through, whichever was appropriate at the time. I remember, during a lunch time, the doctor came to buy a sandwich but I didn't know he was there until I glanced up. I almost passed out! I now know what people look and feel like when they have seen a 'ghost'! I hadn't seen him since the Saturday morning and the shock of him standing just feet away was unbelievable; just took me straight back to finding Tom. He was very concerned about giving me such a fright but it wasn't his fault at all. Bev had seen him enter the shop and was watching my reaction. She offered to take over but I served him albeit with every part of me shaking like jelly!

James had gone back to work in Cheltenham and seemed to be coping all right. He had never been one to open up and share easily and so we could only go on what we saw and what others told us. He had struggled with a number of issues before, and after, Tom's death. We could only pray that he would come through this with a deeper love and heart knowledge of God and His love for him, and that James would experience that love in a very real way that he could take hold of, and run with, for the rest of his life.

Saturdays were a problem for me especially, but also for Alan. I found the time between returning home after three, until about 6pm really difficult and I couldn't understand why. I came to discover that it was, in a way, because I didn't know where Tom was. I knew, and obviously totally understood, that he was dead, believed with all my heart that he is in Heaven but there was a feeling, I suppose, that he *should* have been home, or *coming* home from his Saturday job. After six, these feelings subsided and the evenings were as normal as they could be but we decided that we had to *do* something with that time-walk the dogs or just go out somewhere rather than be at home.

One such Saturday, in early March, I felt so low and missed Tom so much that I wrote a poem to that effect *(Turn the Clock Back – 6th March)* with tears rolling down my cheeks and such an ache in my heart. But once it was written, I began to feel better. God has given me the gift of writing, in poem form, the cries of my heart, whether to God Himself or to Tom. These poems only come in phases and when I am in deepest need, and they speak for themselves. I take no credit and want no glory; I just pray they will touch the hearts of those who read them and in later days will be used to help others who are grieving.

As real as God has been and is to us, the devil has also revealed himself. Alan and James have both (and still do) had times when all they see is Tom, but not alive. James sees him, as he was, on the Friday night and that can come to him at any time but usually when he is driving, presumably because of when he was driving home, knowing something awful had happened but not knowing what. We know this is not of God because of the feelings that accompany the 'vision'. Alan has had the same sort of attacks but worse, and most often in prayer meetings when he closes his eyes to pray.

He sees Tom putting the noose around his neck and going through with the act of hanging himself – the worst thing a father could see. Obviously Alan was not around when Tom did what he did so this 'vision' again has to come from Satan and has been used to prevent Alan from praying. These 'visions' of Tom have happened less as time goes on but they are real, nonetheless.

Satan has attacked me in totally different ways. I don't know why. The first time was a physical attack, at work. Throughout the morning my collar and neck tie seemed to be tightening and although I could easily get two or even three fingers between my shirt and my neck, it just felt tighter. It came to a head during the middle of a busy lunch whilst I made a sandwich for someone. I felt something tighten around my neck – really tight, and pressure from behind as though I was being strangled with a thin rope and at the same time a vision of Tom's face in front of me. As soon as I recognised it for what it was, and prayed, it went. I shared it with Bev, who said I could remove my neck tie and open my shirt buttons, but being the stubborn person I am, I refused to give Satan any chance of a victory and remained 'done up' for the rest of the day – with no more feelings of tightness!

Another time I was attacked came after I had seen our doctor for the first time. He had expressed concern for me to Alan(probably after my reaction in the shop) and said that if I wasn't seeing a doctor, he was prepared to see me as a temporary patient, so I went, feeling fairly comfortable as it was him.

However during the appointment he asked me some questions to which I gave him answers that I thought I had buried and I admitted that I would consider doing the same as Tom (I think really only in desperation and in mis-guided grief that I would see him again – that I *needed* to see him but they were real thoughts nonetheless). I obviously convinced him that I wouldn't do anything like that because he let me go!

He felt that I was sweeping all my feelings under the proverbial carpet, lifting the edge occasionally, deciding that I didn't like what was there and putting it back. He felt I was burying it all in work. (I couldn't *be* too busy, I didn't stand still for a moment, from 8.30am until 5.30pm. I only sat still on my breaks when I coped by praying and did not always take the full time, so I guess he was right!). He also felt that I was hiding in 'church' – not bad for a first consultation!

Anyway, I felt worse during the evening. It was 'homegroup' (one of a small group from church who meet together weekly for Bible study, fellowship and prayer) but I didn't participate much. I couldn't close my eyes to pray because what *I* saw was *myself*, in Tom's room, doing exactly the same as he must have done – really scary or what! I was totally un-nerved by this and withdrew into myself. I cannot remember how I slept or got up the next morning and went into work. Bev took one look at me and knew it was a bad day and I don't know how I got through until break time. She came upstairs with me and we talked it through and how real and terrifying it was. I was so scared that I really *would* kill myself! I worked through lunch and then went home early with Alan, who was also having a bad day but for different reasons. Bev was so worried that she almost called Philip but I said that I would be okay.

Andy and Angela called round on their weekly visit to make sure we were alright and Phil phoned to see if he and Hermey could drop in to see us. God is so good – even now, the right people at the right time! So we had a full house and I tried to brush aside all that I was feeling and I didn't share it, but when Phil prayed it was like he knew exactly what we were dealing with at that time and prayed against Satan and all his 'powers' to leave us alone, in the name of Jesus.

We haven't had any more attacks like that since, but we continue to pray for protection daily. We realise that as we put ourselves in the firing line and tell people of our experiences and of God's powerful hand in our lives and share Him with them, that Satan will not like it and will try anything to stop us.

I have not included these accounts of spiritual attack to in any way give credit to the devil himself, but to show that he is real, and that Jesus' power is sovereign over all and that Satan can, and will be defeated.

On the Monday following, we went into school to speak to the whole of Year 11, at their assembly. We went to thank them for their support; to tell them that what Tom did was wrong. Also we were there to promote the new school intranet site which had helplines available and a confidential e-mail service for those who needed help. We wanted to encourage those struggling with similar issues to talk to someone who can help and most importantly to share again Tom's faith and to pray with them. We were nervous but we knew it was right and that God's hand was upon it. We were backed up by the Deputy Head (a Christian from our church and who had been a huge blessing to us) and there were other teachers present – what an opportunity!

We had prepared what we were going to say and were well covered by prayer on the Sunday in church so we couldn't go wrong really! God is amazing and our words really spoke to those young people. Who knows when they will remember what they heard and be led to the Lord because of it; it was a blessing to be part of it.

We have been – or thought we had been - released by our doctor, who thought we were doing really well. He said that most parents, in our situation, would not be coping as well and would have been on anti depressants ages ago, which is something that neither of us wanted. I can't explain why, but we were adamant that it is not something we would use, or needed!

Alan was on the verge of depression in early March. The doctor told him he was worried. So Alan made a conscious decision to kick himself out of it, and I admired him for it. It was not easy, especially as he had returned full time to a job he no longer wanted to do, but we knew God had other plans for us. We knew that the only reason we were doing 'so well' was because of the constant love and prayers of those around us – near and far – and because of God's strength within us. It was still awesome!

The last thing to share, for the moment, is how God revealed Himself to me in a tangible way, in answer to desperate prayer; how real and how wonderful He is!

Two weeks before Easter, Bev and Paul sold the shop. We knew it was coming but did not expect it so soon. Alan and I had investigated, deeply, the possibility of ourselves buying the business, as we knew it was on the market before Christmas but for some reason I kept holding back. Tom thought it was a great idea and that we'd be good there. Then Christmas came and went and things inevitably slow down for those two weeks. So, we didn't really do much more about it. Then Tom changed everything but we still thought it would be good to go for it – more so because he had thought it a good idea. It was while we were in the shop, picking up the keys for the house in Devon, that God clearly said to me, *"Not here."* So that was that. A door had closed!

So the shop was sold. Personally, I felt I didn't need the emotional upheaval but I would cope with it and support Bev and Paul as much as they had supported me, and so I did.

The new owners were nice enough people but lacking in people-skills and without a clue as to what they were taking on, having never done it before. But that was okay, I was prepared to help, support and encourage them too. However, they made very little effort to get on with me or to get to know me. I was left out in the shop to get on with running it. In fact, they hardly spoke to me much at all and seemed to be avoiding me, which I was okay with as I didn't want to have to talk about what we had been through – although I found out later that they already knew!

Things came to a head the day before Good Friday; I was at a really low point. I felt past caring and I didn't want to feel anything for anyone or anything because it hurt too much. This had been bubbling away for a little while, certainly a few days, due to some things that had been said on the Alpha course. They cast doubt in my mind again, about where Tom really is (God must really despair of me and my silly doubts sometimes) and a letter arrived from someone at church criticising Tom's Thanksgiving Service and the message they believe it gave out. All things have no hold over me now but at the time really served to deepen my sense of despair. (This is why I wrote the poem, *Where Were You?*)

There was a prayer meeting at church on the Wednesday night and I went through the motions, sang the worship songs, prayed, poured my heart out to God but all the time telling Him that I didn't want to feel anything anymore. I didn't care anymore what people did or said. So bizarre really, giving Him my heart, on the one hand, to know and do His will for me but on the other hand almost pleading not to feel emotions that I could not deal with. I remember going home feeling empty – feeling nothing.

The next morning on my way to work, I again cried out to God to help me through, to help me be the support to the new owners, to Bev and Paul for their last few difficult days and be all that He wanted me to be. I also cried out to Him that He would give me something I could hold on to so that I would know He was *real* in those times and to tell me beyond all doubt that Tom is with Him.

So much for being a support to the new people – within fifteen minutes I had written my notice, I just knew I couldn't stay there. However, I am not entirely stupid and I put my notice in my pocket. I thought I would give it to them, see the doctor in my break, who I was confident, would sign me off and not have to work the week. I ran it past Bev, who could see my state, and she ran it past Paul, who said not to give in my notice but to see the doctor, talk it through, and maybe he would sign me off for two weeks which would give me time to reflect – sensible Paul!

Things did not improve during the morning, but thankfully I had very little, if anything, to do with the new people. I found it hard to sell what they were producing; I cannot sell what I don't believe in. It was hard dealing with customers, especially when they asked if I was staying or going.

So in my break-time (and at breaking point) I went to the doctor's, without an appointment but it was the end of surgery so I did not have to wait long. To stop myself crying more than I was I tried to send a text to Alan to let him know where I was and what was happening. But it would not send, so I had to keep trying – at least I was doing something – felt like I was back to needing to do *anything* just to not be able to think or feel.

The doctor called me through – "Jackie,"– not Mrs. Slough - which made me want to cry even more! He listened, asked a few questions, listened some more and decided that it probably was more than just a clash of personalities with the new owners and that it was probably deeper than that, that the time was right for me to deal with everything I had buried for so long. He signed me off for a month.

I went straight back to the shop, gave the piece of paper from the doctor, to the owners, said where I'd been and that I had to go. I left in tears giving Bev a hug on the way and saying, 'Sorry," for doing that to her and Paul.

What does that have to do with my prayers on the way to work? As I was leaving the shop, I was given a parcel by a customer and told to open it when I got home.

When I was a little girl, at junior school, I read a pony story that really spoke to me. I was the girl in the story (and the pictures) and I wanted so badly the things that happened to her, to happen to me too. (I had a vivid imagination as a child, especially where horses or ponies were concerned. They were all that mattered to me!).

Mum started to work at the school, a few years after I had left, and I asked her to find the book for me; to see if I could buy it or at least re-read it but she couldn't find it anywhere. Over the years I tried to find a copy for myself, without success, and without really knowing or understanding *why* I wanted it so much.

Mum tried, unsuccessfully, to find it and James too was looking for it for my birthday. Before Christmas, the lady, from the second-hand bookshop next door, came across a copy (I had forgotten that I had asked her to look) and offered it to me but it cost £110. As much as I wanted it, I felt I couldn't justify that much money. I suggested that we all went halves on it for my Christmas present but I decided that if we had £110 to spend it would be on something other than something that only *I* wanted – especially as I didn't really know just why I wanted it so badly. So I turned the book down and thought no more about it, disappointed though I was.

Well, you've guessed it, my parcel *was* that book. I had been given it and only God knew how much it meant to me; and I have it to look at, to read, and to hold on to whenever I doubt, as real tangible proof of God's amazing love for me.

I wrote, inside the cover, the story of how I came to have it and Alan began to ask me why I had written in it; and stopped himself because he knew that the book will never go anywhere else!

People who are reading this – my God is your God and He loves you just as much as He loves me. All He asks is that you love Him too! Ask Him to reveal Himself to you, give Him your heart and He will always be there for you. You don't have to go through the things that we have had to face but we are so blessed that we have; that He has held us and carried us through these twelve weeks; that He has never left us or forsaken us; and that even when it has been hardest, we have been able to look to Him and praise His name and give Him all the glory and credit that He so rightly deserves.

The second part of my prayer was answered through a lady at church. One Sunday evening the lady I sat next to had a picture of Tom. She doesn't 'do' pictures or visions but she is a godly lady whom I respect. Her picture was of Jesus in white and Tom arriving before Him, also dressed in white. Jesus spoke to Tom, who draped himself across Jesus' knee as only Tom could. He said, "You've come sooner than I expected; you've come too soon but I am so glad you're here." And with that they got up and walked off together.

The lady tested that out with God and shared it only when she was certain that it was what God wanted us to hear and in His timing, which in all things is perfect. I heard what I needed to hear when I *needed* to hear it, and I received His gift of love when I needed it most.

Alan also had a picture of Tom, whilst driving one day, soon after. He often thinks of Tom as he drives and he often wonders what Tom *does* in heaven all day (as you do!) His picture was clear – Jesus was teaching and Tom was in a group, leaning forward on his chair, joining in and asking Jesus questions!

So, what is it like living without Tom? I was thinking this morning that we have seemingly, very quickly, got used to him not being here. I used to think that it felt 'right' that he wasn't here, in a funny way. I felt that we three were as we should be. I think now, that it is because he hasn't 'gone' in the sense that people, without faith, would see and grieve over but he has just gone on before us to that place where all believers will one day go; we shall see him again when we meet with Jesus face to face. And we know, through the visions that people have shared, that that place is real. It *is* as it is promised in the Bible.

But it is still a much quieter house without Tom; no banging doors; thumping down stairs, bursting into a room, and so much tidier without loads of books lying around or so much washing to do. I get half the hugs and half the compliments that I used to get. Do I want him back? No, I just want those precious memories. He is in a far better place, safe from all his inner pain and torment that he hid from us so well. School days still hurt, when the bus goes past at ten past four and he doesn't get off it. And the dogs still bark once as they did when he walked down the drive. We still obviously have a lot of grieving to do ourselves (if we would only give ourselves permission!) but we will come through. God has good things for us to do with all that we've experienced. I remember someone saying, one day, "Who else would He have trusted with all this?" One day I will ask what she means but I hold on to it for now and it gives me strength.

You think that you're doing alright, that you are coping well, not crying so much, especially in church – that got a bit boring after a while. I mean, *every* service, morning and evening, during the worship – but they were healing tears and we couldn't help them. So, now when we haven't needed to cry for a while, along comes Easter Sunday, two baptisms and we're back to square one! We thought we would be emotional because Phil and Hermey's daughter, Caris, was baptised but it stirred up memories of our own baptisms, on Easter day, and also that before Caris, Tom was the youngest Philip had baptised. So we didn't cope with that day too well but it shows that we're not there yet. There's a long journey ahead but it is exciting to walk it knowing just *who* is holding your hand!

Things that are just ahead are a quiz night for Tom's friends – to thank them for their love and support. Also the inquest into Tom's death, which we don't know how we will cope with but we pray that it will be easier than we fear; as most things have been so far.

May 2004

It's hard to believe that I wrote all the above only three weeks ago; so much has happened!!

We held the quiz night for Tom's friends, which went well. There were only a dozen or so but they were his closest friends so that was good. We had questions, then a break for pizza and cake and then more questions and prizes. We ended the evening with a message (of course) which was something Tom had written last year, entitled 'INRI'. Alan had power-pointed it and set it to *Turn your eyes upon Jesus* which is a beautiful, emotive piece of music.

<u>INRI</u>

Four letters
Who knows what they mean?
Who knows what they stand for?

You know.
Somewhere in your distant memories.
Look back to the end of each school year.

Those services ....
You never concentrated.
You always used to look at the pictures.

The windows.
The life of Christ in glorious stained glass.
His life. His death.

That's it?
INRI, above His head.
The sign hung above Him on the cross?

That's right.
But what does it mean?
Jesus of Nazareth, King of the Jews.

Well done.
But it means much more.
To me, it means so much more.

What then?
It is His crime what He died for.
It mocks Him with the crowds.

What else?
It is more than mockery.
It is the truth of Jesus' mission.

His mission?
Jesus is not only a man.
He is God's son, the Christ.

We know.
But you don't <u>understand</u>.
Jesus died to save <u>you!</u>

Save me?
He died to save you.
He died because God loves you.

INRI
Four small letters, seemingly insignificant
They stand for Jesus, for God

INRI
What does it mean?
What can it stand for?

For YOU?

Turn your eyes upon Jesus
Look full in His wonderful face
And the things of earth
Will grow strangely dim
In the light of His glory and grace

We used it once at a prayer meeting in Moreton so Tom had actually seen it and approved it. But it really spoke to those friends and was an emotional time which, actually, we had not intended as we wanted the whole night to be fun.

Unfortunately, once we got home, the rot set in! It hit hard that Tom was not there and never would be – but you pick yourself up off the floor and carry on with living.

The next day was the Alpha Course 'Holy Spirit' day – a whole day given to explain the work of the Holy Spirit and His relevance to peoples' lives today as they seek to follow Jesus. We were there because we had been helping to lead a table of people during the course. There is a prayer time, which normally I would go for, but I felt so emotional, after the quiz, and I did not want to cry in front of anyone, so I didn't go. Alan did go for prayer and Daniel prayed with him. Dan had a very strong sense that Tom's death and our grief would not be the centre of our story but that there was a bigger story to follow…This made sense to me and was a comfort.

We had to see the Coroner's assistant on the Tuesday, which was tough but necessary. Again, he was as gentle as before and prepared us fully for the inquest the next day. We were really unsure of how we would cope or how we would feel afterwards. It seemed like it would be the closing of a chapter of our lives that we could draw a line under and move on; that was what we thought…

<u>Wednesday 28<u>th</u> April</u>

The day of the inquest into Tom's death – and only twelve and a half weeks after he died! We had been told, at the time, that it would be at least six or seven months. Even the coroner's assistant was surprised but we felt it was all in God's timing and in His hands. We felt quite calm. Lots of people were praying and we felt carried again. James had decided to come with us which was brave but good and we felt we were three 'in this together' again as we had faced everything else before.

The Headmaster from school came too, in case anything 'sensitive' came out that could upset Tom's friends. But the coroner made it clear that although he had everything Tom had written – in terms of letters and his 'suicide file', he was not going to disclose any information from them. Praise the Lord because that was our fear and the reason the Head went. The whole thing lasted twenty five minutes and was very sensitively handled – his verdict was that Tom took his own life by hanging, which was the truth obviously, but there were so many horrible ways he could have said it.

So that was that! We had prepared a press statement which we gave to the two reporters who were present and who followed us out wanting to ask us questions. We felt relieved that it was over and that it hadn't been as bad as we had feared and felt quite positive.

Over the evening, however, we began to feel low. In fact we did not go to homegroup, which is unheard of for us, but a bottle of wine and a video helped a little and we slept well.

We had a very busy day next day, with visitors and preparing Alpha food, so we didn't have time to dwell. The papers came out – the Gloucester Echo was nicely written – a good headline – the coroner's summing up and verdict in full – as was our statement and they had printed Tom's picture, which I thought they might. We had really hoped for just a small column and no picture but it was nearly half a page. The Cotswold Journal on the other hand was not so nice, which was a shame as it is a more local paper and the one all Toms' friends would see. Their headline, *Tom, 16, leaves Suicide Mystery* and if they could mention suicide or hanging as many times as possible, they did. They did not print our statement in full and put the verdict as hanging; and again included his picture and took up half a page. Still, at least it wasn't the front page this time.

On the Friday night, there was a quiz night at church, which we went to, and then we went up to the school, where Tom's friends had organised a gig, with six live bands, all from within the school. The school had never allowed anything like it before but it was held in memory of Tom, so with great trepidation the Head and his team gave the go ahead for it. The kids did a great job organising it all and sold two hundred and twenty tickets. There was no trouble at all, even though the school had provided security men, and we went for about the last half hour – it was great, but LOUD!! But it set me thinking again, being surrounded by Tom's friends, listening to his sort of music, that there was so much more I should have been for him, as his mother. It was late when we got home – almost midnight – but I had the lines to a poem buzzing around my head, which had to be written – the one I called, *Guilty?* It summed up exactly how I felt at that time, like so many of my other poems and which really wrote its self. And again, the pain of being at school and coming home to a house without Tom, all led to a really low weekend, another chance for Satan to strike.

On the Saturday evening after 9pm Alan and I went for a walk around Moreton. We were both feeling 'down' and a walk seemed like a good idea. It was good to get out and into some fresh air and just to be able to talk about mundane things. We were okay and just walking single file along the narrow pavement towards the school steps when a huge lorry came over the bridge. It took my whole attention and things seemed to go in slow motion. I found myself thinking how inviting and how easy it would be to just step out in front of it and it seemed to pull me to it – whether the darkness of the night and the brightness of his lights made a difference I don't know – but time just seemed to stand still as it came towards us.

I had to physically turn my head away and shout at myself to stop me from doing what Satan wanted – I certainly did not want to end my life, and not in that way. I made myself think of Alan behind me and

James and also the lorry driver and I was so relieved when he drew level and it was too late to step in front. I did not tell Alan – I was scared to, although when I did tell him about it on Sunday, he said he too had felt something evil when he saw the lorry but dismissed it.

I did not have an opportunity to tell Phil until Sunday evening, by which time I was quite worried and scared by what I had experienced. Phil was great, and took me seriously, and we decided that as I personally did not wish to die, (I was grieving for my son, which was understandable and my doctor and I agreed not to give me anything but time) that we would tackle this thing through the power of prayer; and that it was purely a spiritual attack and not a mental state.

I was operating the sound desk that night but Phil said that when he gave the opportunity for prayer at the end of the service, to let the sound look after itself and go out for prayer!

Well that's what I did, except I almost didn't go (Satan again). Bearing in mind my poem from the heart about not being able to let go and cry, as Phil prayed, that Satan had no authority over me, and then about letting Tom go, the floodgates opened and I couldn't help myself. Alan and James came and sat with me and we held each other as people prayed for us. It was a really special time. We all felt it and I knew God's peace in my heart again. I know that the times when I feel low are the times I have to be on my guard, to seek God's face and to learn to recognise spiritual attacks, to be able to rebuke them, before they get a hold on me. Its great to be in the battlefield. I must be doing something right for God, otherwise Satan would leave me alone!

June 2004

Wow! God is awesome and amazing that He would take our situation and ourselves, just as we are – still hurting, still grieving, but still praising His name and seeking His face wherever we go – and give us a future full of hope and joy and so many opportunities to share with others…

Way back – two years at least –a friend shared a dream with us. She saw us both very clearly working at The Riverside Christian Centre, not as volunteers but in a management capacity. We were all still 'baby' Christians then and didn't know enough of visions or prophesy to recognise it. I wanted a coffee shop but had no funds and we were alright in our jobs (though not really happy). So we put it out of our minds and dismissed it as a nice 'dream'. I remember after an Alpha talk, on guidance, I almost shared it with Phil but wasn't confident enough and couldn't see how it could happen anyway!

At the same time, unbeknown to us, Susan and Molly (the managers) and everyone involved with The Riverside were praying for 'the right people' to come; to be a part of it all and to continue it when Susan and Molly were no longer able.

As I mentioned earlier, we had been drawn to The Riverside since Tom died, initially to 'be' as it is such a special place, but one day I felt a need to go there to 'do.' I had such a strong feeling that I had to be there to serve. Once I was signed off from work I went a few times to help out, which was good but I always came away feeling I could have done more and that there was more for me to do. I shared with Susan, telling her I wasn't doing enough!

While we were away in Devon, at the beginning of February, we felt that it would be a good idea to run a Retreat Centre, alongside the Christian Coffee and Bookshop that I wanted. (I had had an aching desire for my own Coffee shop for a few years, only since becoming a Christian in 1999, never before) but we couldn't see how. It would be a huge financial step so we sort of dismissed it. Alan carried on investigating different catering premises in Moreton that we could operate as a coffee/book shop, none of which I could get excited about.

Meanwhile thoughts of The Riverside Christian Centre kept coming into my head. I thought it would be ideal but couldn't see how it could happen (all this time, Susan and Molly were on the other side of the world in Tasmania. They had been told of Tom's death by people from their church but we had had no contact with them. In fact, we hardly knew them. They went away just before Tom died and were gone for five weeks).

I shared with only three people – Phil, the friend who'd had the 'vision' those years before, and Helen – my thoughts on a coffee shop/retreat centre and they each agreed that The Riverside would be perfect. But there were obstacles, such as no accommodation and no salary. So whoever works there has to be self-funded. Nothing is charged for, except by donation or whatever people can afford and everything is given in Christian love. And we really did not know Susan and Molly that well, but we thought them to be ladies of God. So we stopped thinking about it but it wouldn't go away. Because God had so clearly said, " Not here!" in the teashop in Moreton, I was expecting Him to tell me that The Riverside was right – kind of "It's HERE!!!" and each time I came away, after helping out there, and He hadn't spoken to me, I felt disappointed.

It was the first time we saw Susan and Molly, once they were back, that Susan said, "Who else would He have trusted with all this?" Now I know what she meant! Before they came home, at the end of their stay in Tasmania, Susan said to Molly, "Alan and Jackie will be joining us at the Riverside." I don't know what made her say that but it's amazing anyway!

We didn't want to say to them what our thoughts were (in case they thought we were stupid) and anyway there were still those obstacles to overcome – at least, the accommodation and self funding – and I was still waiting to hear God's voice. They didn't really want to share their thoughts with us, as they were waiting to see if we would approach them. So we invited them to dinner, thinking it would be a good opportunity for them to ask us to join them because that might just be the way it would happen – that God would speak to us all. As it happened, that was the night Susan shared her vision of Tom meeting Jesus and it was absolutely right that nothing else was discussed.

Eventually, the week before the inquest, Philip told us to stop messing about and go and talk to Susan and Molly about The Riverside. So we did. They listened and asked us questions which we answered honestly, about those obstacles, and we admitted that we didn't know the answers but it still felt right to be there. Susan shared what she had told Molly in Tasmania and went out to make coffee in the kitchen – where she proceeded to dance with joy and was still singing and dancing days later! We then had to meet the Trustees of the Centre, who would have the final say, which Susan said would be a formality. This was arranged for the 7th of May, which was also the day our house went on the market!

I had felt strongly, for a long time that we were not living as we should with regard to our finances and the preaching of recent weeks was speaking volumes to me and also to Alan. When I suggested that we sell the house and clear our debts and move to somewhere smaller, he agreed. We had not seriously considered The Riverside Centre at this point. All that was still in my head and my heart so, after sharing with Susan and Molly, we went ahead and put the house on the market – knowing there was nowhere for us to live at The Riverside, at the present, but being certain it is what God wants and knowing He will provide, so long as we are obedient to Him (a word from Philip, given to him by God, for us).

We met the Trustees – and they gave us a good grilling! It was much tougher than Susan had suggested but also really good and powerful and confirming that God was in charge. They sent us out for a coffee so they could talk about us and – having said at the beginning that they might need more time to reach a decision, called us back in and said, "Welcome aboard!" So that was it. It can now become official!

We began to share the news with people from church and almost, as one, they said, "You are exactly the right people," which has been a real confirmation of God's hand upon everything as that was the prayer of two years previous. We feel it was really confirmed when we told our families, as they are all behind us one hundred percent; being totally aware of all that is involved, especially from the financial aspect but also from the living by faith and stepping out in total trust, which we were really excited about! It is a huge leap of faith for us but we know God has carried us through so much already and He has so much more He wants us to do; and we want to do so much more for Him because we love Him so much.

So the things we see as obstacles are not really – they can be overcome. There *is* somewhere to live – its just not available just yet and Alan will have to drive for 2-3 days a week to provide an income but there is so much potential to continue God's work at the Riverside; so much has been achieved by Susan and Molly through their vision and their faith and by God's provision. I feel so humble at times to think that we have been called to such a place that God wants to use us there and whether we, or especially I, will be up to the task, sometimes it's overwhelming – we have been Christians for such a short time (November 1999) and we have so much to learn.

James is happy about the changes and he will be off to Aberystwyth in September. Our thoughts, right now, are to buy property there that he can live in and rent out a couple of rooms to other students, as the house prices are about what we will be able to afford once we have cleared our debts.

It has all been a whirlwind of emotion. I have been signed off all this time, and it has all happened so quickly. We have been concerned that we are riding on the emotions surrounding Tom's death and our grief. But it is not *because* of what happened that we are doing this but because of what happened we have been released to be *able* to do it, as Tom has been released from all his suffering, which he hid so well from all of us.

We still miss him terribly. I long to turn the clock back and still I ache sometimes from missing him – it is a physical pain and it seems to be harder to bear as time goes on! I worry that I have forgotten what he looked like and yet, sometimes, I cannot bear to look at his photo. I long to touch him and hug him – or have him hug *me* the way he did; and also sometimes I long to have him there to shout at, to tell him to come in *quietly*, or stop picking his nose, or tidy his room. It hurts when

I see or hear young Christian men praying in church – when I think of all he could have become for the God he loved so much.

All these feelings, I suppose, are normal. It is only seventeen weeks since he took his life and yet so much has happened – sometimes I want to scream, "Stop the ride, I want to get off!" I am learning not to fight the tears – especially in church but at home, also, they seem to come when I least expect them, or when I have made up my mind not to cry, or during Sunday evening, or special prayer times when I think I want prayer for our future and end up crying for our past. But God is in control and He knows there are more tears inside. He knows when and how to release them. This time will pass, but we have to come through it as part of the healing process and our journey with Him will be all the richer for it.

I am about to take control of a situation that has controlled me for so long. I am about to write my notice for the teashop and a weight has been lifted from me. I'm still not sure I am strong enough to hand it in personally but I feel a peace about doing it. I only have two more weeks before I have to go back and I never wanted to go back. It felt like the scariest place on earth, having been, when Bev and Paul were there, a very safe place to be. It feels good to take charge instead of just 'seeing what happens when the time comes'.

I feel I have so much to learn. I am not the most confident person and I feel I cannot relate to others very well or hold deep or lengthy conversations, especially in the company of other Christians, who know so much more than I do, even if they are younger than me! But I realise it is a journey we are on and we are given opportunities to learn as we go. I look at ladies half my age with so much more confidence than I could ever hope to have, doing so much more than I have ever done, and I think, what a lot of years I have wasted, and what a lot of time I have to make up for. But I know that God will use me and the things we have been through in positive ways in the future. We feel that we would like to share through public speaking and through enabling other grieving parents to spend time at the Riverside Christian Centre, to experience God's healing and love in that place and just to be able to reach out to those who pass by and call in for coffee, to gently share God's love with them – so many opportunities and such a mighty work that needs to be done. We feel so blessed and privileged to have known God more through all that we have experienced. We could so easily have walked away and turned our backs on Him but that was never an issue. From the very moment of finding Tom, realising that he was dead, and phoning Philip first before anyone else (apart obviously from the emergency services) we knew God is above all and it was to Him that we cried for ourselves and praised for taking Tom's hand when he needed Him most.

I have had two 'pictures' that I would like to share. The first was after the trustees meeting when we were praying with Susan and Molly and was of a great volume, leather-bound and gilt-edged. The pages were turned back, signifying the past few weeks since Tom died. And a fresh page was opened and ready to be written upon, which is our future. The second was of a four legged chair with a leg missing, which was Tom, and a three legged stool, which is capable of carrying great weight, which I took to mean that we three must grow together and learn to support each other and move forward together.

A year later I found this in a book by J. John:

The assurance of our relationship with God is rather like sitting on a three-legged stool. When all three legs are there, we are secure. If only two legs are there, we are a bit wobbly and if there is only one, we are likely to fall over. The three legs of a Christian are:
1. The Word of God – the Bible.
2 The Work of Christ – what He has done for us (on the cross)
3. The Presence of the Spirit – who lives in us.

All three are needed for us to be stable Christians.

Part of Me

Part of me is missing
And can never be replaced,
How do I cope with the living
And face what needs to be faced?

All of me is hurting
My heart is filled with pain.
How do I face tomorrow
When I'm living yesterday over again?

Part of me is struggling
For the son who is still here,
How do I show that I love him –
When all I want is for Tom to be near?

All of me knows I'm their mother,
And I'm still a mother to James,
How do I cope with the feelings
Of love, fear, guilt and shame?

Part of me knows he's a man now,
Who has his own life to lead,
How will I cope when he leaves home,
Will my heart once again start to bleed?

All of me is scared right now,
Of the things that lie ahead,
A whole new way of life for us –
Is that where we're being led?

Part of me is doubtful –
Whether I'm up to the task,
How will I be all that I should be,
For the things that I'm being asked?

All of me knows it is God's will
It is what He has called us to do,
He will help us as He tells us
"My grace is sufficient for you".

Jackie. 28. June 2004

Father God

Father God will you hold my hand
As I walk this walk with you,
Will you lead and gently guide me
In all that I say and do?
Will you bless me and encourage me
When I do just what you say,
Will you pick me up and hold me
When I stumble along the way?

Father God will you speak to me
In the times I cannot hear,
Will you open my eyes and ears to you
Make your voice so crystal clear?
Will you point me to your Scriptures,
Help me read them everyday,
Will you bring your word alive to me,
So I see what you want to say?

Father will you wipe the tears from my eye
As I pour out my heart to you,
Will you fill me with your Holy Spirit
And in your love please make me new?
Will you give me just sufficient grace
To live each day for you,
So I can make a difference Lord
And to your heart stay true?

I only want to do your will
And seek your loving face,
To know when I am doing right
And to rest within your grace.
I trust you Lord with all my life
I give everything to you,
I know that in the hardest times
Your love will pull me through.

I know that I am weak my Lord
And I fail you again and again,
But by your strength I will be lifted up
And I will praise your Holy name.
Oh Jesus, help me find the words
To say all that I want to say,
My heart cries out – I need you Lord
Help me live for you today.

Jackie. 29. June 2004

I wrote this letter to Tom, one day, when I missed him so much. It is self explanatory. I would recommend any grieving person to do the same. It really did help.

As the days go by and reality sets in, we remember things you did – the way you'd burst through a door (you couldn't come through quietly). Sometimes you would apologise but mostly you'd just burst through as loudly as possible. I see now it was your way of getting attention – even if it was negative, and we told you off. Sometimes it would make me laugh, the way you thumped down the stairs and into a room but all the time you were screaming at us to notice you and to say something; but you were screaming in your head and we didn't hear you – we thought you were okay.

Playing on the playstation or the computer, we didn't want to interrupt you; you were always so involved in the games and listening to your music in your room – isn't that what we did at your age? We thought you were okay. You'd help us when we asked you to – we would talk while you dried up. (You would always ask, *"So, how was your day then?"* – did we ever ask you the same?). We'd tell you we appreciated what you did for us – the dogs and jobs around the house but we never said we appreciated you. I would say, *"Love you"* when you went to bed but did it mean enough – with everything else in your head. I wish I'd told you how proud I was of you more often – how good looking you were, those gorgeous eyes, even your longer hair (I was coming around to that), your lovely quiet smile, I couldn't believe you were mine sometimes.

Sometimes I would 'hurt' with love for you. I couldn't understand where that came from and I never told anyone. I should have told you. I can understand your physical pain, the things you've written about because I've sort of felt it too. I wish you had opened up to me – but would I have really listened or would I have heard what I wanted to and butted in with my point of view, like I know I did?

I'm so proud of the way you never let on how much you were hurting inside – you were such a good friend to them both. They loved you too but how I wish you'd spoken to me. We could have prayed it through each day but God knew and He loved you more for it.

You were so strong in your faith. That has been an inspiration to me since you died; the debates you had at school and the way you stood up for what you believed in has influenced a lot of people and will continue to do so.

I wrote the above shortly after you died – on the 27th of February – it is now July and I still miss you so much. Sometimes it feels like it all happened to someone else, like it never really happened and you will come home or I will wake up one morning and find you in your bed. I was praying this morning and asking how it could be that you felt so desperately unhappy; that all you could think of was to take your life. I am so very sorry Tom that I was out all day at work; that I was not here for you when I should have been; that I put other things before you. I am sorry that I compared you with James – you were so different but my only experience as a mother was with him first and he was so easy. I was hard on him too. Maybe you didn't see or know that but I worked on the principle that if he came through things so would you and if something was good enough for him it was good enough for you too –and that meant in going without certain things too. I didn't know any different.

I am sorry for all the times I laughed at you – I should have told you it was because I loved you so much for who you were. The night before you died we laughed at you because we thought you'd made toffee sauce and eaten it all yourself. What must you have thought of us? And when you lost the house key and even when you fell down the stairs – it just seemed you could do nothing right and yet you were doing everything right and I should have told you.

I hope you are watching us. I hope you realise how wrong you were about us. I pray that you can see what you meant to us and how much you still do mean to us. I know in my heart that you are doing great things for God. I just long for the day when I can see you and hold on to you for eternity and tell you how desperately sorry I am for all the hurt I must have caused you. I wish I had been a better mother – you deserved the best and all you had was me.

Sometimes I re-live the moment when I found you. I want you to wake up and smile at me and say you just dropped off – and we can laugh and start again and put things right and make everything better. I am not writing this so you feel sorry for me. I don't want that. I just want you to know that if I could change things I would.

We are moving on. We have grown so much closer to our God who showed you so much love and it is because of you that we have that knowledge of Him. He has held us and carried us all this time and has led us to a new direction in our lives.

We will always love you, Tom, more than you ever knew. Thank you for the privilege of being your mother.

God bless you.

See you later.

xxx

June 2004

An annual prayer day was held at The Riverside Christian Centre each June and this year Alan and I were helping out with organising the day. It gave us a good taste of what we thought we would be involved in once we moved there.

It was a really good day with over sixty people in the morning and just a few less in the afternoon session. The Morning Prayer time was concentrating on 'Riverside people' (key folk involved with the day to day running) and revival. When it was our time for prayer as 'Riverside people', Susan asked Alan and I to stand at the front and she asked Philip and the guest speaker to pray for us. It was a special time. We had had no thoughts of Tom – we'd been too busy setting everything up. But, as usual, our hearts were touched through the worship time and as Phil prayed, for ourselves and for James and all that we have been called to do, he included Tom in his prayers and we both just broke down. We each tried to fight it as we felt embarrassed for the people who didn't know our story but then we each just felt it was okay to let our emotions be seen as it was such a special time and God was with us.

The speaker said, in his opening prayer, that he did not know us or anything of what had happened but as Philip was praying he had a clear picture of a ship going through a dark and dangerous storm which lasted a very long time. But as it was tossed about by the waves it was led towards a lighthouse which shone very brightly and so guided it to safety. As the speaker gave us this picture I felt very clearly that that had been Tom. We were reminded of the story that Philip read at the Crematorium service about a ship disappearing from view only to be seen over the horizon by other people as it came into their sight. (We were given two roses by different people in memory of Tom and we found two planters with a picture of a ship on them to remind us of that story.) I felt that Tom was the ship. All that he had felt through his life and had battled with and kept hidden from us, (only ever giving us answers that he knew we wanted to hear and not what was going on in his head and that he knew God's love more than he knew ours), I felt that, for him, God was the lighthouse shining from heaven to guide him away from this evil world that Tom thought was dragging him down. (Certainly in the last six months of his life that was what was happening) So now Tom is shining up in heaven in peace and safety. That was what I felt during the prayer time but also I can see that we three are that ship; that God has brought us through a tough and stormy time into the peace of his harbour; that we can be the lighthouse, shining for His glory, by the telling of our story and sharing of God's love with those who come to The Riverside.

July 2004

Well things are progressing. We have had two prospective sales on the house, both of which have fallen through. We have just this week found a perfect house in Aberystwyth for James, an unbelievably good buy. God is so good! We just pray that we can hold on to it while we try to sell this one. There are still no earthly signs of a property for us at The Riverside but we guess that God needs a little more time. We have a peace about the whole situation and trust in the Lord completely as He battles on our behalf. Molly received a scripture to that effect – *You only need to remain calm; the Lord will fight for you.* "(Exodus 14; 14 Youth Bible*).*

I have been busy helping most days at The Riverside and Alan is working hard. It is James' last day for his job in Cheltenham today and he is looking forward to some well deserved time out! I am in a difficult position job-wise as I really only need work for a short time. I really don't want to work at all. I would rather spend time at The Riverside, where my heart is, but financially I need an income until we sell the house.

We have had good days and bad days, again both at the same time; it is good to share with others who say they feel the same – Mum and Helen particularly. Father's Day was a tough day for Alan. James bought him a good present and card and we went out for lunch. Last week was tough on each of us; no reason that we could think of, except that we were really tired and we seemed to have so much to deal with and so many decisions to make: house sale, house buying, planning for the trip to Romania with the church to support the charity that we have links with, me deciding whether to go or not and the short time scale of everything. I just felt I couldn't cope with it all.

But this week has been much better and I feel back on form! Tuesday was when we found the house for James and we put an offer in on

Wednesday. Their agents spoke to our agents and they are all happy even though our house has fallen through. Praise God it doesn't seem to be a problem.

Today has been a blessed day for me. I was going to The Riverside but felt ill when I got up so I called Susan and stayed home. I had a strange feeling I should be home; that I should spend the morning in prayer and cry out to God to confess my sins and seek His face. I felt it was what He wanted from me. So I did – I am learning to be obedient, I think! Anyway my prayers turned to Tom and I confessed how I felt I had let him down and prayed that he was listening and would know how sorry I was. I then finished the letter I had started in February to Tom and in it told him all that I felt.

I couldn't settle to anything so I sorted out a cupboard and found photos of the boys as they were growing up and also school photos that I thought were lost. I realised as I was doing that that I felt so close to Tom; it sounds corny but I felt warmth and such a different kind of peace and of love and a real sense of his presence as if I could just turn round and he would be there. I feel that he understands and that he knows how much we love and miss him. It brings me close to tears as I write this but I did not ever want to forget the experience – it feels like God really heard me this morning and sent Tom to me this afternoon and that was why I had to stay home; an awesome experience that makes me trust God even more. I don't know if I will ever have that feeling again but it was enough to be given it today and that is why I had to write it down.

The Battle Belongs To The Lord!

I'm locked in my mind
Full of guilt and fear,
Where are You Lord
When Satan's so near?

Will You keep me safe,
When I'm too weak to fight?
Will Your angels surround me
Keep me safe in Your light?

Lord, unlock my mind
Set me free from despair –
It's when I can't see You
I need to know You are there.

That's when it's the hardest
To look up to You,
To take my eyes off myself
And look to Your truth.

This battle I'm fighting,
It's You who must win,
Though Satan surrounds me
I will not give in.

I'll give You the glory
And praise You deserve –
I give You my life Lord,
It's You I will serve.

Jackie. 21. July 20

Depression?

It's like this black cloud that surrounds me,
Invades and takes over my mind,
And the things people say – though I know they are true
I deny them time after time.
I feel helpless and hopeless, unworthy and weak
Locked in my mind, unable to speak,
Full of pain and anguish but most of all guilt,
And God's far away – I can't lift my eyes,
They're fixed on myself and this wall I have built.
Satan is happy, he's winning again,
Keeping me down, enjoying my pain,
Telling me things I don't want to hear –
But it sounds like the truth and fills me with fear,
For what I might do, one day in my life,
To make retribution and everything right,
I won't speak it out as it gives it authority
But it seems, in the blackness, a real possibility.
Satan shows me the way, how easy it is,
Whispers quite clearly –you don't want to live.
Oh – but I do, help me Jesus, give glory to You,
To win this battle – to You I'll stay true.
Slowly but surely the cloud goes away,
I get on with living, face each new day,
And most of the time, when life seems a doddle,
All the above is a load of old twaddle.
But I never know when the cloud will come back –
When Satan is poised for another attack,
It comes from nowhere, right out of the blue,
Most unexpected, what should I do?
Hold tight on to God's love and live in His grace,
I know the answers – look to His face,
But Lord, it's so hard to cry out for me –
I can pray for others, their needs I can see,
Teach me Father, what I should do –
It's not about me, but all about You.
I give You the things I hold dear in my heart,
I give You my life – set me apart
To serve You and love You for all of my days,
To worship in wonder and beauty and praise,
For You are the one who created us all,
You are the one at whose feet I will fall.

Jackie. 22. July 2004

<u>30<u>th</u> September 2004</u>

Where to start! The last two months have been really tough for me. In August I wrote some points down of things that had happened so I will start with those and hope to make sense!

House: Our sale fell through and so we had to re-market. It fell through a week before we were due to exchange contracts and Alan had a difficult time trusting and seeing God's hand. All he could see was wasted time. We had to pull out of the Aberystwyth house sale and he became frustrated that time was running out to be able to buy a house and settle James in before the start of Uni.

We decided to apply for halls for James and to look for a property later. We can see now that it was the right decision and that our good God has gone before James. In his block of eight rooms, three are occupied (including himself) by students from Campden school who knew each other. Also, a guy, whose brother is a flatmate of a friend from the CYFA Christian camp that the boys used to go to at Sparkford and made many friends, e-mailed James to introduce himself and to say that he is in his third year at Aberystwyth and attends St. Michael's church, which has a really good ministry for students. He took James to a bonfire and BBQ on the beach, on their first night. It really helped us to know that God had put these people in place and made leaving him there much easier but more of that later before I jump way ahead of myself and miss out important things.

Back to July…Alan was off to Romania on the 26th. James spent two weeks in Cornwall with his school friends, had a great time and came home two days before Alan left. I could not decide whether to go or not and was really torn. I got to a point where I mentally could not make a decision and in the week before Alan went became quite depressed, to the point of spending two days just sitting and unable to move, feeling totally locked inside my mind. Alan was very concerned, and considered staying with me and not going to Romania – which he was torn about anyway but he made us an appointment to see Phil, which I grudgingly accepted. I had written some thoughts and questions down which I needed answers to, although really I knew them anyway. So we went and spent time with Philip, but I wasn't honest with him because I knew if I said what I was really feeling, Alan would not go to Romania. I knew that he needed to go and that I needed the time with James before he went to Sparkford camp, and then the time on my own afterwards, which I was scared about. I was feeling so low that I was worried what I might do. However, after our meeting I felt a poem coming on… and that was when I wrote *Depression?* which was exactly how I felt, but again, once it was written I felt a release and knew that I was going to be okay.

So Alan went to Romania. James and I spent a week together and then he went to Sparkford 2 as a Taskforce Leader, for ten days; something which he had very mixed feelings about, going without Tom.

We had been in contact with the camp leader and expressed our concerns for James and said where we felt he was at. We were encouraged that they would look out for him. Also, we knew that it would be a blessing for James to go and be among friends of his own age.

It was a time of testimonies. Susan had asked me if I would give a testimony to a visiting group, which I did. It was tough and I nearly threw my notes at Susan and told her to do it when I got to the 'Tom' bit. I just wanted to run out of the room! But a deep breath and a prayer for God's strength kept me going. I think it blessed people, as many of them came up afterwards and shared that they had lost family too and that it was only with God's love that they had come through.

Alan was asked to share his testimony in Romania with Ecce Homo and their families, on the Sunday morning, and he said it was tough and there were tears. But it was good to be able to share with God's people who have been praying for us since January.

James was asked to share his testimony with the other taskforce leaders on camp; something he really struggled with but he was so honest about where he was with God that it touched many hearts and enabled him to draw closer to God again. It has been so hard for him to see God's hand upon him; he feels far from God a lot of the time and struggles to know of God's love for him.

I had a good week on my own and felt stronger for it – I wrote this down in my notes so I will copy it here:

'I was feeling like the last six months hadn't happened. In a weird way I wanted to hang on to the painful memories so I don't forget Tom. I'm scared I've already forgotten him when we plan for the future etc. so I want to re-live 30th January because it was the last time I saw him – even though he was not alive – but I realise I need to let go; it is time; he is safe; God has him!!!'

That must have been after I finished the letter I had started in February and after the wonderful sense of His love and presence that I wrote about before.

The house was sold and the people wanted to move in within two months but we had a bad feeling about the purchasers. They really haggled about the price and let us down several times over viewing. They were actually one of the first people to come and see it back in May. Anyway, they let us down once too often and when another couple offered a little more money. We said, "Yes." This was a couple who saw it also in May but were unable to proceed because they had to sell their own house; but when they came to see it, Alan immediately thought they would be the ones to whom we would sell, but he kept quiet as we had other people interested. The original purchasers then offered us the asking price, which we turned down, much to their surprise. They couldn't see that it was not about the money – the lady actually came to us one evening and offered to do a private deal and offered even more money, which we still turned down.

So there was great excitement. We were going for a four-week exchange and things were progressing well – right up to the day of exchange when the buyers at the bottom of the chain (only three buyers in the chain and the bottom people were first time buyers so seemed the strongest link) pulled out. That was on a Friday and a difficult few hours – God where are You in this? Are we meant to be going to the Riverside? Are we doing something wrong? Questions followed. Then we took our eyes off ourselves and looked to the experiences of others and thought who wants to stop us and for the first time realised that the promise that God had given to us in June, through Molly, *You only need to remain calm; the Lord will fight for you.* (Exodus 14v14 Youth Bible), was a reality so our trust returned. On Monday the sale was back on, as new first time buyers came forward for the house at the bottom of the chain, with funding in place, so delaying things by only a few weeks. As I write this we have heard nothing to the contrary so assume all is going ahead. We still do not know where we shall be living at The Riverside but are praying for a house on site so we don't have to store furniture or dogs!

We planned a farewell BBQ, for James the Sunday before he left for Uni. It was to be a surprise for him and we invited about fifty friends and family. He decided, however, to go to London the day before to stay overnight with friends as they were holding a BBQ down there so we had to be a little devious in our encouraging him to be back for 1pm for his party which he knew nothing about!!

We told him that Mum was planning a family lunch and so Alan picked him up from Moreton station. Then he pretended that I was calling from Mum's to say that she needed milk and oranges. He couldn't think of anything better! James called in to Budgens to buy them, went to Long Compton where my parents live and before turning into Mum and Dad's road. He suddenly 'realised' he was supposed to pick up a pudding from The Riverside (no surprise to James as he knew I had made one and taken it there to freeze). So he came to The Riverside with an unsuspecting James, who only thought that Mum would be getting a little cross if she had planned lunch for 1pm.

They pulled around the back of the building so James would not see the tables and chairs in the courtyard and stopped outside the conservatory, which is when James wondered what was going on. He assumed it was a group booked in – until he realised that he knew the people inside and that they were there for him. His face was a picture and his comment to Alan, as he stepped out of the car, "My brain can't cope with this!" Well, he hadn't got to bed until 5.30 in the morning!!! It was a lovely time and worth all the planning and preparation (and secrecy!). So it was good for James to know that there are people here who love him and are supporting him in prayer as he enters a new chapter in his life.

As I said, at the start, it has been a really tough two months for me. I have needed to talk but have not felt like talking. I have felt guilty for not working for an income. I have been full time at The Riverside, which I felt was right. However I felt that instead of getting out of debt, I was contributing to it. I also questioned myself about whether I was 'hiding' in The Riverside because it was a safe place. I still do not know the answer to that one but I know that it has been such a blessing and a privilege to be part of everything that goes on and to learn the basics before we start full-time.

Susan and Molly have been so encouraging and so welcoming and I know I have taken some of the load from them. There have been days when I can't wait to get there and days when I don't want to be there (when I don't want to be anywhere). Yet, within a short time my heart is at peace again and I know it is God's hand pulling me through. My big concern is that I get so involved with what needs to be done that I forget to spend time in His presence. Yes, I send up short prayers but I don't spend time with Him.

I want so much more from my relationship with Him. I want to become all that He would have me be so that I can be for others what He needs me to be. I feel so frustrated because when I read the Bible it still doesn't make sense sometimes. I want to hear from Him that He wants us at the Riverside, that we are doing what He wants and not just what seems like a good idea. I'm frightened that when we move in, God will move out because we are so inexperienced. At the same time I know we are going as 'practical and hands-on' people to release Susan from those responsibilities, so we can learn from a spiritual lady. Even when I ask God to speak to me I don't seem to be able to hear Him.

I read wonderful stories from godly people and testimonies of how He speaks to them (I am reading *Miracle Valley* by Jim Wilkinson, WOW!) but why won't God speak to me, even a little bit. I want the best for Him; I pour out my heart to Him. I sing worship songs with tears pouring down my cheeks because I love Him so much and I feel so unworthy of His love for me. Sometimes I cry because of Tom but it's more than that. So why can I not hear Him? Why does He not hear me? That's when you wonder if you really are a Christian, if you really did give your life to Him, if you didn't do it properly when you asked Jesus into your life. I sometimes wonder if He accepts other peoples hearts and lives but not mine – and yet I do know He loves me and He has spoken to me, twice, and each time I did what He said and I do trust in Him but sometimes it is so HARD !!

Gosh! Where did that lot come from! This is supposed to be an honest journal from my heart and especially my journey through grief and the ups and downs of this year. To be honest, there have been times, over the last two months, where I have felt my writing to be be rubbish and twaddle and worthy only of a bin or bonfire but I will keep on with it – Alan will not let me throw it away anyway!

I have been very tired – mentally and physically, since mid August. I put it down to needing another B12 injection, which I have every three months but have still felt tired since I had it. I am quite fed up with everyone telling me I look tired and pale. It is one thing feeling it without being told you look it. My ambition, now, is to look radiant for the Lord (I told Him that this morning, when I *did* spend time with Him). It is more than being tired from hard work, as I wake up refreshed, but by the time I have done the dogs and had breakfast I am ready for a lie down! So I know everything I do at The Riverside I do in God's strength, because I certainly cannot do it in mine!

I have seen my doctor this week and am awaiting blood test results. He has already made his mind up that I am depressed – and perhaps I am but I do not want any happy pills. I still do not know why not; it is not as though God has said do not take them; it is just something deep inside that I do not want to do.

Campden church was flooded in August – we had some awesome storms while Alan was away in Romania and so through September we held the evening services at The Riverside (my suggestion and I knew Susan and Molly would jump at the chance, even though it meant extra work for us).

Anyway, during the last service, we felt the Holy Spirit move amongst us and I felt a lifting of pressure off me, as though I had been held in a vice. I felt free to really worship the Lord, such as I hadn't been able to do for a long time, and to rejoice in His presence. Since then I have not been so mentally tired and weighed down but I still feel physically tired. I guess that even though we are at peace about where we will live, trusting that God will provide (even if at the last minute) and looking to Him for the sale of the house and to watch over James, and all the day to day things that we are involved in, there are still pressures as we naturally question what we are doing. We face the fact that it will be hard work and feel the frustrations of just wanting to be there and get started. Now that James has taken his car, I have to rely upon a lift each day and I hate that – being dependent upon others! I have borrowed a bike but don't have the energy to ride it. It is six miles. I might only do it once but I am determined to do it! (Postscript – I never did!).

Anyway, we will wait for the blood test results and see what the doctor has to suggest next week. I know I should ask for healing but I don't know how and we pray for people with life-threatening and incurable things within our church so what is a bit of tiredness or depression within me …?

Why is it that we (especially women) find it so hard to ask for prayer to be healed of something we consider as 'minor'? I have just spoken with a good friend (it is July 2010) who has had the most painful ear infection for over a week, which involved being sick and passing out and just living for the next painkiller. As friends, we have prayed for her and at a church meeting over seventy folk prayed. One of our Ministers visited her the next morning to pray for her healing. She was already much better and out of pain, having slept soundly all night and woken feeling fantastic! He asked her why she had not asked for prayer or for someone to visit and anoint her with oil and to pray for healing. She replied that it was 'only an ear infection' and not life threatening.

As soon as she said this we were reminded of what I had written above. Friends, if God loves us as He says He does then, surely, He wants the very best for us. He wants us to be fit and healthy, not burdened under unnecessary pain. He doesn't cause our illnesses. They are just a part of life but He wants us to be free from them. I have realised that it is not a sign of weakness to ask for prayer for something 'trivial' but a sign of faith and maturity. We stand before God our Father and ask for His healing, in the name of Jesus and through the power of the Holy Spirit. Remember, it is the devil that makes us small and encourages us to think we are not worth it but, by golly, we most definitely are! Also what parent hasn't held a hurting child in their arms and longed to kiss away their pain. How much more then will our heavenly Father want to do the same for each of us, His children? *"Ask and you shall receive."*

But you do have to ask.

Birthday

You should have been seventeen today,
You would have been driving your new car,
Instead of which, you're with our Lord,
Watching over us from afar.

You had a lovely birthday Tom,
All your friends were there,
Bringing flowers and a seat in your memory,
Showing how much they all still care.

We spent the day visiting James,
With my parents so we'd all be together,
We ate good food and raised you a glass –
It was a day to treasure forever.

And now we're home, your Dad and I,
Now the tears can begin to fall,
Even though we know where you are,
We're still trying to make sense of it all.

Sometimes I wish I could die instead,
As if that would somehow bring you back,
My heart is broken – there's a Tom-shaped hole.
How will I ever get over that?

I should look forward and focus ahead,
To the time we'll see you in Heaven,
But it's hard to let go of the hurt and the pain,
When it's with you twenty four seven.

And yet, we know you're having a ball,
Doing great things in heaven above,
Our hearts rejoice that you're free from your pain,
So today, just receive all our love.

Jackie. 20. October 2004

October

I am actually writing this in January 2005, after a particularly difficult weekend, when I felt so far away from God that I could have just walked away from what little faith I have – but I didn't!! I'm still here. Such a lot has happened since I last wrote in this journal; some things I wrote down at the time and others at the end of November; in note form so I wouldn't forget. So if things are jumbled and don't always make sense that is why.

Picking up from where I left off … Rob and Marion White, from Mainstream Ministries, (they were speakers at many of our annual church 'weekend away' breaks and are very special friends of Chipping Campden Baptist Church) came to The Riverside Centre to speak to a group and then to lead our service at CCBC the next day. Knowing how much they care and how much sense they make, I really wanted to speak with them but because we were so busy, we didn't have an opportunity to do anything more than just exchange pleasantries and small talk. Come Sunday evening I was desperate to speak with them as I had cried out to God to speak to me through Rob or Marion but I was in such a poor state of mind that I felt, a) that I was wasting their time, b) that I didn't know what to say or how to say it and c) that they couldn't possibly have anything important, especially from God, to say to me at that time.

In the end it wasn't until we were leaving the church, after the evening service, and nearly everyone had gone that we were able to be on our own with the two of them. I can't remember what was said, except that Rob just said to me, "You have so much to give but don't be under any pressure to give it," and "You don't think very highly of yourself, do you?" Rob couldn't have known the low opinion I have of myself; only God knows how hard I try for Him. I have felt so worthless for two months and have tried to keep going, all the time questioning myself and God, and desperately needing His love and reassurance which Rob was able to give me at that point. It probably doesn't make sense that what Rob said could make such a difference to me, unless you know Rob, but just by his being there and caring I felt lifted up and strengthened.

That was on the 3rd of October. James was home for the weekend and drove back to Aberystwyth on his birthday, the next day. I spent the week crying out to God that I did not want to be depressed and that I did not want to have to take pills. The last time I saw the doctor I felt he had decided that this time I would need medication. I was also scared that he was right. Anyway I breezed into the surgery feeling on top of the world and told him truthfully that I felt fantastic. My blood results were all good and he felt that possibly I had had a virus. Alan 'went down' with something viral three weeks after coming back from Romania and was not at all well for a while. I blamed it on the Tripe Soup and said it served him right – I mean there are some things that you don't need to experience to get the flavour of a country!!

On the 12th October some of Tom's friends called round for the evening. It was good to see them and to catch up with all their news, how they were doing, GCSE results, etc. The same evening, as I had been waiting for them to arrive, I was flicking through the property ads in the local midweek paper and a house jumped off the page and hit me!

It was a colour photo and the price looked good. I really only looked at the prices first as we couldn't afford much and we were still looking in Aberystwyth for James. After the boys had gone I casually showed the ad to Alan, saying that was the kind of thing we should be looking for. He agreed and we arranged to view it the next afternoon at 4:30pm.

So we travelled to Bidford on Avon, saw this little house which we fell in love with and both felt that we could live there – although the plan was to rent it out. We put in an offer on the way home and waited to hear from the agents the next day.

I was working at The Riverside and Alan was driving. He had a short day and arrived to meet me in the afternoon, looking sheepish, so I knew he had agreed a price on the house – but he did want to confirm it with me. Another offer had been made which was lower than ours and we were advised that if we came up with another thousand pounds the seller would include all carpets, curtains, dishwasher, washing machine, cooker and hob etc and that she would also pay the stamp duty. So we said, "Yes!" And then I worried that it was all too good to be true. Too quick – a temptation from the devil. Too good to be a gift from God (how could we deserve such a thing?). It had only been on the market two weeks and it was its first week in the paper but the seller wanted a quick sale – which in fact took only four weeks and three days from viewing to completion!

As I write we are still awaiting tenants but trusting the Lord to provide!

Tom's Birthday

A very special day and one which we did not know how we would cope beforehand but, as with all the difficult days, we felt God's hand upon us and felt carried in prayer.

Tom's friends wanted to mark the day and so we arranged to meet them up at school at 9:00am, where they presented a bench in memory of Tom, which they placed outside the main entrance. Then we all made our way to the top of the Manse garden, where they wanted to place flowers. There were twenty six from Tom's year and it was a very moving time.

Alan tried to say a few words, but struggled with emotion to find the right ones, and then we put our flowers down – roses from bushes that we had been given, in Tom's memory, back in February and that had given us much pleasure over the summer. Then those friends (who had bought their own flowers – some arrangements that they had signed cards for and some just a single flower) and also a small fire engine appeared from somewhere. To this day we don't know who put it there but we love it and cherish the love behind it.

Then we all went into the church, where Philip made tea and coffee, and we were able to spend time with the kids, some of whom went back up to the garden for their own 'time with Tom'. After a while we left everyone there with Phil (who was brill and spent time chatting with them). More came at lunchtime (those who had had lessons in the morning). It's a measure of Tom's personality that so many wanted to come; we were really moved.

Mum and Dad had come with us and were 'blown away' by the morning. We hadn't told them about the bench, just about the flowers. We wanted them to be surprised and blessed, which they were. We had a good journey to Aberystwyth, except that I remember going into a petrol station and while Alan was filling the car up with fuel, Mum and I went into the shop to buy sweets for the journey and the guy behind the counter said to me, "Cheer up, it might never happen." Let me say he was very lucky to still be standing…! Please don't ever say that to anyone – you never know why they look sad or what their circumstances are.

We travelled uneventfully on to Aberystwyth and met up with James and had a really good evening, with dinner, in a fantastic hotel and raised a glass to Tom.

Mum showed some photos that we hadn't seen, of when the boys were younger, and it was a lovely evening. We stayed overnight in the hotel, spent some time with James in the morning and came home in the afternoon. As usual, it was when we were on our own again that it all caught up with us and I wrote Tom's birthday poem, straight from my heart as I was feeling it.

So, that was 20th October and we were moving house on the 1st November so lots to do – packing and arranging – etc. We decided to move ourselves and Alan was about to enquire about hiring a self-drive van when he bumped into a friend at the garage whilst filling the car with petrol, who said we absolutely must use her horsebox, for which we are so grateful. We packed all Tom's things together from his room and just stored them with everything else. In fact it wasn't until two moves later that we felt able to sort them and pass some things on and dispose of others. There are still some bits that I don't want to decide about yet so they are stored in the garage and when the time is right we will deal with them. I remember thinking sometimes, "Well, it was his choice to die, so he won't mind us throwing things away," which sounds really callous and hard but just sometimes that's how I felt.

James came home to help with the move and to say goodbye to the house, for a proper closure. And so we started to move on Friday 29th, taking some things to The Riverside, expecting to only move into a bedroom and bathroom in the main house and finding that Susan had rallied everyone the day before and cleared the upstairs office. So we could have a sitting room of our own and be self-contained, apart from a kitchen.

They all worked so hard on our behalf, it was really humbling, especially as Pete and Steve (two guys who did a lot of the manual work there) came to pick up the dog run panels and a lot of heavy garage stuff early Friday morning, having been sworn to secrecy about our accommodation. So we knew nothing about how hard they had already worked for us until we dropped the things off to store in the outbuilding. We found there was very little room because all the office stuff was there!

Saturday, we loaded the lorry again with all the stuff that was to be stored in a different location. Sunday, we took a day off for church although we still did bits – last minute packing and cleaning etc. and then on Monday, we moved.

The money transfer happened mid-morning and we gave the keys in afterwards, and that was that. We spent eleven years in that lovely big house that God found for us before we even knew Him. We had had good times and some rough times. It was a good place for the boys to grow up in and the place where we learnt of God's awesome love for us when Tom died but strangely it was easy to leave. It was just a door closing and no looking back – just looking forwards to a new future together with God. Philip and Helen came to pray after James had left for Aberystwyth and we just really prayed for the new people and gave thanks for our lives there and prayed for our new life at The Riverside Christian Centre – a good and special thing to do with special people.

Our first week in our new home was good; we settled in really well and took gentle jobs to ease ourselves in. Pete and Steve were still really busy on our behalf, creating luxury accommodation for the three dogs that were to live outside – they have never had it so good as is evident by the way they cannot be bothered to leave their straw bed or heat light to say goodnight, or even good morning. They used to have the same comfort at Moreton but this is obviously so much better!!

Our first night was spent looking for Monty, who had gone missing from his temporary home. We had just finished a lovely 'welcome to your new home' dinner when the phone rang and we were told Monty had gone a different direction to everyone else on his evening walk and now was missing. So we dashed off to search the fields and hedges in the dark around where he was staying, with no luck. So we abandoned our search, until morning, feeling fairly calm. Monty is a sensible dog and probably found somewhere warm and cosy to hole up in until it got light and he could see where he was going – which seems to be what he did!

Helen picked me up first thing (Alan was working) and we went to the farm where he was staying. I looked around the fields – no point calling him as he is deaf – and Helen walked down the road where Monty just trotted up to her from nowhere and sat down, a little muddy and hungry but otherwise perfectly fine. We brought all three dogs home with us that evening and they have settled really well.

There seemed to be something on every night that first week – prayer meetings, our church homegroup in Moreton and the Alpha course at CCBC which kept us busy and gave little time to adjust properly.

People asked us on the Sunday at church how we were settling in and we truthfully answered, "Really well," and that it felt like we had always been there. I remember someone saying that was the sign of God's calling, and that it was obviously right.

Then we had a difficult week. Alan had gone back to work. Susan did not seem to be able to think straight or make a decision. I suppose it was sheer exhaustion and relief after all the hard work to move us in. No-one really knew until just before we moved where we were going to live and people were still praying for the provision of our own house on site. But we recognise that we have very many lessons to learn, to cope and adjust to living with others, when we are not really 'people' people.

I felt alone and that I was meant to be Jackie, Alan and Susan all at the same time as well as coping with grief and major upheaval. We had a big weekend group to prepare rooms for and plan menus for, a Saturday group and Molly's 91st birthday party to boot! I had a huge wobble and felt convinced that it was all a huge mistake and not what we were meant to be doing at all. Alan calmed me down and made me see that Susan was not her usual self and we worked things through and everything turned out okay. The groups were all catered for and Molly's party was a success. I guess I was trying to do things in my strength and not calling upon God's strength, so things just got all out of proportion.

During this time, I had glanced at the stars one evening and they seemed so far away and I felt that was how far I was from God. One Sunday evening, while walking across the yard by myself, I looked up and the stars seemed really close, as if I could just reach up and touch them and I clearly heard, or felt, God say, "That's how close I am to you." That brings a lump to my throat as I write this, knowing God's wonderful love for me and yet still not believing He could think me worthy of such love. I am reminded each time I look at the stars, of that night. I pray one day I will believe it without question.

James came home for four days. He has a room which he can call his own. He said it felt a little weird sleeping over there and spending time with us upstairs in our flat but that it still felt like home.

I cannot make head nor tail of my notes from now on. It all seems a bit jumbled and I cannot remember what caused me to write the next bit but I know it was as I felt it. We were approaching December and I was feeling 'strong in the Lord', which was good. Alan was frustrated at having to drive a lorry for five days each week when his heart was to be at The Riverside and to support me. In these times I felt 'I was being us' and couldn't cope with the responsibility. We decided that we could afford to pay the mortgage for three months on our Bidford house and that we were trusting God for a tenant. Alan started to drive for two days instead of five which was much better for me and gave us enough income to cover what needed to be covered.

We had to start making decisions for our first Christmas without Tom. We had to decide what we wanted to do and where we wanted to be but not knowing how we would feel or cope. I had to think about sending Christmas cards to all our puppy owners from the days when we used to breed Border Collies and to our relatives and friends. I really could not face the task. I remembered something Tom said last year, when I could not be bothered to send any because I was so tired from work. I was just sharing that with him and decided that I should make the effort and send them (approx 60-80) because they would give pleasure to those who received them, to which Tom just agreed. But it was the way he said it and looked at me that stuck with me. Maybe he wanted more of us than we gave him; we were so busy giving our time to others that we didn't give the boys the time they deserved. But James was working and independent and it was just Tom stuck at home on his own so much. Neither of them complained so we didn't realise. We would try to encourage Tom to come with us but I guess that was not an option for him. I used to worry that I was working too much and that he had too much time on his own, after school, weekends and a lot of evenings. At least in the holidays he worked a lot, but I couldn't think how I could change things – you get in a vicious circle with loyalty to your employers and the more money you earn the more you need because it still wasn't enough to pay the bills (it seemed that way anyway). I should have put Tom first instead of my job. I don't know if that was behind the way he looked at me, perhaps its just hindsight. So Alan wrote a letter giving our change of circumstances and mentioning about Tom; and also mentioning God quite a bit; and I wrote the cards and posted them. We had quite a response from people who did not know and some who we thought we had told. At least it was an opportunity to 'speak God' into people's lives at that time of year so it was good to have done it.

I will copy this next bit as it is important,

"I am learning not to feel guilty for feeling really happy – we have moved on and Tom is safe. We cry for ourselves and for our loss; also I cry when I think of how he must have felt to do what he did; in the hours and minutes before; and all I wish I could have said and done – most of which I've written in this journal. We don't want Christmas; just want to hide away and let it pass; want to celebrate the birth of Jesus and that is all."

Christmas Eve 2004

When I was a little girl Christmas Eve was to me like a fairy tale, so special and magical. All the preparations were done, the house was decorated and the presents were under the tree. My sister and I were allowed a 'grown up' drink and would go to bed and sing carols before falling asleep. As I grew older the magic was still there. I would stand at the window and look up at the sky, waiting and full of wonder, not knowing why I felt like I did; it was much more than the excitement of opening presents. I couldn't describe it then and I still can't describe it now but over all the years it never left me, even more so when the boys were little; I would feel it for them.

As the boys grew up and we made our own traditions – we had a pop-up book of the 'Night before Christmas'. James would sit on one side of me and Tom would sit the other and we would read and lift the flaps and they would take it in turn to shout out the word underneath, sometimes deliberately wrong-guessing from the picture on the flap and we would have a big finale with the words, *"Merry Christmas to all and to all a good night,"* which we would shout in unison and loudly! Then they would have their own 'grown up' drink to help them off to sleep sooner so Santa did not have to stay up so late (I needed my sleep!). This all got trickier as they got older and stayed up later and by this time they were just humouring me as they knew who Santa really was!

Two years ago I was woken by Tom, who was being Santa for Alan and myself – I remember I screamed the place down as I woke to find a 'man' by my bed. (If I am woken by an unexpected alarm, be it clock or fire, (or person) I am very dangerous – just ask Alan!!)

We really appreciated what Tom did – even if I did give him the fright of his life. He left presents and a letter each, to the best Mum and Dad. He was just so generous and amazing to think of doing that for us. He did it last Christmas as well but this time he left the presents by the bedroom door – so as not to wake me I guess! And this time he didn't leave a note, such a shame. Alan decided that I wouldn't do the book this year. It will be put aside for James to read to his children.

As Christmas day has got closer it has appeared to be a huge mental monster from which there is no escape – which we do not want to face. So many decisions – where to go, what to do, to do what we want, or do what we feel we should. In the end we decided to be here at The Riverside Christian Centre doing and being what we needed to do and be, and James knows that too. If we all cry together that will be good; if we all laugh together that will be great but none of us knows how we're going to feel or react.

As tonight approached we had decided to go to Stour Valley's Christmas Eve service, as there wasn't one at Campden. As it got closer I did not want to go – and I was right, as I cried through the whole service. Alan wept too! We left straight afterwards as we just could not face people and be sociable.

I feel, writing this, that the magic has gone out of my Christmas and that no Christmas will ever be the same again, however hard we try to recapture the old 'wonder of it all'. I know Tom is having a great Christmas with Jesus so I guess my tears are for all Christmas's past and for feelings that will never return, and as for tomorrow, the day itself, that is something to be faced after a good sleep and with God's help. We are at peace with putting ourselves first and doing what we three need to do to get through and we know we will be carried by the prayers and love of so many good friends.

James is sleeping on the sofa – his choice so we're all together in the morning. I have bought him a new stocking to open from Father Christmas so that it will be different from the ones he and Tom used to have.

Susan and Molly have been so fantastic. They have just listened and been there; not pushed or intruded at all. It has been difficult for them, as they have had a Christmas to plan for as well.

I wrote the above straight after the service, when I wanted to capture how I felt. Alan lit a roaring log fire and we spent the rest of the evening with Susan and Molly, watching a film until late, so that was a different way to spend Christmas Eve and it was good. I put James' stocking on the sofa, while he was in the bathroom, and he gave me such a hug when he found it. It meant a lot, that I had done it that way. I suppose he must have wondered what we would do; we both nearly cried; it was a nice moment. Then we all went to bed not knowing what tomorrow would be like.

Christmas Day 2004

Our First Christmas Without Tom

We got up, as normal, did the dogs and went to church! James had opened his stocking and it was just good to be together. The service was lovely – full of fun and laughter, as it always is on Christmas morning. I remember Philip saying on our way in, that it was a day for Jesus and so I determined to put Him first and my feelings second, which I think was what Phil meant. He knew how we were feeling and said just the right thing to take our thoughts off ourselves and Tom and to focus them where they should be – on the Author and Perfector of our faith.

After church, we came home and spent time with Susan and Molly before they went to lunch with family. It was a good time; we felt relaxed and comfortable. Whilst our lunch was cooking, we opened some of our presents. We felt awkward to begin with, as the boys had always given out the presents from under the tree (as my sister and I had done) so I gave the dogs their presents, which took away the awkwardness, and we each took it in turns to take a present and open it.

Christmas dinner was good – as always Alan excelled himself! It was about mid afternoon, by this time, so we fed the dogs and walked them, opened the rest of our presents and spent the evening in front of the telly watching Harry Potter and thinking good thoughts of Tom!

We went to Mum and Dad's for lunch on Boxing Day which was lovely. And on the Thursday evening went back for an evening meal at Mum's with my sister and her family, again a good time, although, I think we were sub-consciously helped by the fact that Ashley was not there – he is six months younger than Tom. It made it not so obvious that Tom was not there and I suppose we could ignore the fact that he had died and imagine – not consciously – that he was with Ashley in another part of the house – strange how your mind can work.

Susan and Molly went away for a month, from the Friday, something they do every year to recharge their batteries. We knew how much they needed the break and they knew how much we needed them. They were very concerned for our well-being while they were away, to the point of almost not going. However, we took them to the airport and waved them off and the rot didn't take long to set in!

Every New Year's Eve Philip holds a communion service. This is such a special way to see in the New Year. We remembered that, last year, Tom had wanted to go and we were so pleased as we thought he was slipping away from church. It was becoming something of an issue, especially to me and through January, as I felt, but didn't understand, something very sad and heavy in his room. So, when he wanted to come to the service, we were just really pleased for him.

We went this year, remembering last year, and feeling the loss so much, especially after Christmas. I am afraid we cried through most of it. Afterwards everyone hugged each other, which was tough as we really wanted to run away again but every hug was given to us in love and compassion and was special; and we needed and appreciated every one of them.

We opened the Coffee Room, at the Centre, the next day (Saturday) and as it was quiet we sat and added up the stock-taking figures. We began, I suppose, to feel the weight of responsibility, without Susan there, but we were doing alright. We closed early and went back over to the house. I was feeling low by this point and, by accident, whilst looking for something for Alan, found something that turned me upside down and inside out and back again. I will not say what, as it is personal between me and Alan and we have since talked the issue through but at the time I retreated into myself and became locked in an inner turmoil. Alan did not know what had happened to me and could not understand that I could not speak of it. If I did not understand my own reaction, how could I explain to him how I felt?

We had an uneasy night. I did try to explain myself and Alan apologised and I understood his intentions and admired them but it did not change how I felt about me.

Sunday morning and we hardly spoke. I did not know what to say. We just did the dogs and jobs between us and got ready for church. Once there, things did not improve. I could not pray before the service; couldn't feel God there at all. I put the songs on to the church computer and as people arrived, especially friends who asked how I was, I knew I could not cope. So I grabbed my coat and left. I walked up the High Street and out of Chipping Campden, around Dover's Hill and back into Chipping Campden – quite a walk really! But I just put one foot in front of the other and plodded on, feeling bad for leaving church but knowing I couldn't have stayed; knowing I couldn't go back until everyone had gone home after and feeling so miserable; knowing God was there, but feeling so far from Him. I was feeling surrounded by blackness, hurt and pain, feeling like the one person I trusted most (Alan) had kicked me when I was already down but not being able to explain why – still even to myself. I felt something of what Tom must have felt and that bought its own pain. I felt guilty that I was not praying for those friends who were praying for us. I felt useless and wretched and all this was locked in my mind and I could not escape it.

I hung around the car for a bit and walked a bit more and eventually Alan found me and we went home. I made lunch for us and James, still not talking and just getting more withdrawn. At some point, in the afternoon, we did talk and I shared a bit of what I was feeling – what was easy to talk about, nothing too deep – and so we went back to church for the evening service at least talking to each other. Alan knew it was not him that I had the problem with, it was me but he did not know how to deal with me and neither did I.

I decided to sit at the top end of church, on my own, so I could run out if needed and spent the time reading anything in the Bible that would get me to hang on to God – Psalms, Isaiah 40 – anything I could read through my tears. Several ladies came to see if I wanted them to sit with me and were obviously concerned but left me where I was (but I know they were praying for me). I knew what the sermon was on as I had put the songs onto the computer and I knew I had to stay and hear it. It was Hebrews – *'Hanging in there with God'* – just for me or what! By the end of the service I was cried out and able to sing the songs and mean what I was singing and I felt better, although I still could not speak of what was in my mind. I did not know how to or who I could trust as it was stuff that was buried so deep and I felt I had trusted Alan and he had let me down, even if he meant well.

By the time we came home, we were talking and I continued to feel better and we had a normal Sunday night after church – home by 9pm, light meal, do the dogs and go to bed.

The Coffee Room was open the next day and there were people in to look after it so when Philip called in, saying he was 'just passing', we were able to have a coffee and a chat. He was obviously concerned for both of us and we talked about Tom and how we were coping with grief at that point. It was a tough time on the Tom front, never mind The Riverside front and the 'me' front! I was seeing dead people behind every closed door and having panic attacks where I felt something bad was going to happen and I couldn't stop it.

I remember one evening going into the Coffee Room to fetch something and someone had left a book on the table, which had not been there earlier in the evening. (There was usually a Bible Study group that night which was not meeting because of the Christmas holidays). I just freaked because I thought that whose ever book it was had turned up for the study, found no-one there and gone into the next room and hung themselves. I totally expected that's what I would find if I looked into the next room. But I made myself just go straight back to the house and told myself it was stupid but real nonetheless.

Alan finds the time keeps replaying in his mind when he came upstairs in panic at my crying out to him and finding and trying to revive Tom. I remember the operator telling me to tell Alan what to do but I kept saying it was too late, Alan was doing everything right and I was watching – watching him do chest compressions, knowing Tom was dead. I had the easy job, being on the phone, so it's not surprising that that is what haunts Alan the most. I guess he feels he should have saved him but he couldn't have; no one could.

Anyway, Philip prayed for us and left but I knew I should have said more about what was still locked in my mind. But I didn't as I felt I couldn't in front of Alan and I simply did not know how to or where to start. The Coffee Room was busy with lots of people coming to see how we were so I didn't have time to dwell and I hid it all and put on my happy face. I can act quite well when I need to!

Alan was driving the next day and I felt quite panicky. I did not know what jobs to do, felt I would be wrong whatever I did, although there was no one there to judge. But I knew I had to do something so I made up some beds that had been used and cleaned the room. As I was doing this, I thought of an expression that Philip had used to describe how I had appeared on Sunday. He said, 'my fur was ruffled' and I thought it was apt and began to think about why I felt the way I did. As I thought, I kept getting the same lines over again so I found pen and paper and the poem, *This is Me Right Now*, poured itself out in about five minutes. I didn't think about what I was writing down or whether it rhymed or not; it just seemed to spew from deep inside. I had prayed over Christmas that God would help me to write a poem expressing my feelings but I didn't expect that one!

Usually with each poem, once the words are out, I begin to feel better, but this one was different as I knew it was stuff and feelings I had buried since my childhood and through our marriage, right up to the present. I knew I was going to have to face what I had written and deal with the issues that had surfaced. There were things I had done that I was ashamed of and I confessed these on my knees before God and asked for His forgiveness and help to move forward. I have never been able to talk about myself. Everyday thoughts and feelings I could express, but I cannot let anyone get to the real me. I immediately put up walls and go on the defensive, feeling sure that they won't like me or they'll think I am stupid, because of the answers I give. So, I suppose, I build a barrier to stop the conversation, so I don't get hurt and nobody wants to talk with such a prickly person, so they usually change the subject and move on to someone much nicer. (I have discovered that when it's a tough 'Tom' day and it's hard to talk because you know you'll cry, that if you smile and swiftly say you are fine and turn the conversation to the other person and everyone in their family that you can think of, that they will think you are okay and go away quite happy because you've had a nice chat!!)

This Is Me, Right Now

My fur is ruffled, I feel cold and exposed,
Trapped in my mind, I feel so alone.
One minute I'm angry, but I don't know who with,
The next I'm so scared I don't want to live.
I need to talk, but I can't even do that,
I feel useless and stupid, ugly and fat.
I don't know me and I don't like who I am,
I don't see who others see – to me it's a sham.
I know who I want to be, but it's just an illusion,
The real me is lost in guilt and confusion.
I've been a bad mother and an even worse wife –
Selfish, self-centred, that's been my life.
I don't know how to give anymore –
If there's anything left to pick off the floor.
I'm desperate inside; on the surface I'm fine,
Don't worry about me – it's not the end of the line.
I'll do what I need to, keep up the act,
Keep pretending the truth and hiding the facts,
But God knows my heart – there's no escaping from Him,
Lord, I know You are there, let Your healing begin.

Jackie. 4. January 2005

I was still 'locked' into my mind and more so now that I knew I had to deal with what was in the poem, and I hadn't a clue how to. Alan read it but, bless him, he didn't know what to say or do so we didn't talk much about it or where it had all come from. He felt that I should see a doctor, but I felt, and still feel, very strongly, that God is holding my hand and that, however tough and painful, I have to go through this time, in order to grow and become strong to do what He has called us to do and I will come through. He showed me this by pointing to a little book called *Coping with Depression* which I found when it leapt off the shelf at me. I thought it wouldn't do any harm to read it, to see if I was depressed or not, thinking not. And it was amazing – written by a lady G.P. – who has had depression and treated lots of people with it and written in a no-nonsense, no-guilt way. As I read it, I thought, "Wow, that's just how I feel so many times." It was really eye opening, but in a good way, as it made me see that I am okay really. She says that not everyone needs medication; some just need time.

During a Sunday evening service, our last song was *There is a Day* and as we sang it, Phil had such a clear picture of Tom, just another confirmation that he is happy and we will see him again. I gave Philip a copy of the poem saying it cost a lot to share it – he knows the poems are healing and that they only come out of heartache.

Sunday 18th January Alan and I led the morning prayers. Alan had asked to, as it was twelve months since we had last done it, when we had prayed for God to help us as a church prepare for 'change' as that was what Alan kept feeling God was saying. And there were a lot of changes expected that year –we were to plant a new church in Bidford and within the music group, as people left to go with the plant. There was a calling for a new Director of Children's Ministry across the churches. We did not expect the change to be so evident in our own lives and in such a huge way!

Anyway, we led the prayers, during which I prayed for parents and children and the children's workers as I felt led to. Alan spoke a little and prayed a short prayer and introduced Tom's 'INRI' to encourage people to think about Jesus. Then we sat down and 'INRI' started. There was supposed to be a short pause for reflection afterwards but people were so touched by the music and words that nobody moved –God's presence was tangible. We looked around, as we were waiting for Daniel to get up and preach and thought he might be waiting for a cue, but everyone was praying. It was a special time; Tom is still reaching people through that message. He has touched so many people in his three years of being a Christian, more than most of us touch in a lifetime. People who knew him will not forget him and people who never knew him, wished they could have met him. Maybe they will one day! Daniel eventually got up to preach, deep in thought and prayer at what he had seen and told us, later that evening, that he was deeply touched and that it was a special message. Most people, who knew Tom and us well, thought it was one of Toms', although we had specifically not said so at the beginning.

The next evening was a 'prayer for healing' meeting at the church, so we went, not to be prayed for, but to pray for others. It was the fourth time we had met as a group and so we shared encouragements, hearing of those who had improved since the last meeting. It is good to be encouraged. So often we want to see instant results and we desperately want to see miracles in those we are praying for so it was good to hear that God is at work and answering our prayers. There were about twenty of us there that night and Philip asked those who had come for prayer to raise their hands so he would know who they were. He asked someone to play the piano while he anointed and prayed for people.

I was praying and then found myself listening to *Lord I come to You,* which was my baptism song. I was lost in the music and thinking about the words and what they meant to me that night, when I was aware of Alan sitting next to me. We had been sitting apart, as Alan had led the worship time to begin the meeting. Philip was in front of me saying he wanted to anoint us both and pray for us. Well I tried to fight the tears. Alan was crying next to me and I kept trying to push my tears deeper inside and not let them out but as Phil prayed, they just came, and came, and still came, and then even more. I felt desperate, desperate pain, like nothing before, pain from the feelings that my poem brought out but most of all Tom pain, that he shouldn't have died, that he should still be here. I so badly want him here; I want all the pain to stop but more than that, I want never to have had the pain in the first place. I was aware of the people in the group but I just could not stop crying. I know I was not just sobbing gently but I guess it was a healing meeting and that's what God was doing inside me as I had asked him to. I wasn't surprised that Philip had prayed for us. I felt that he might, as I had asked God what I should do with all that was surfacing and all the emotions that were buzzing around in my head.

The next day, Alan called in sick to work and we spent the day together, not really doing anything much, but we both felt emotionally and physically drained. I felt that it had not been good to cry, that it left me feeling worse but over the week, I have felt much better and calmer. I still have moments of sheer panic and times when I cannot make a decision but Alan and I have become closer and I feel I can share some of myself when I make a discovery about why I feel how I do or what makes me do certain things.

A big thing was being able to share with him about what I wear – or can't wear – especially to church. I have hidden behind a big jumper and jeans a lot lately, not wanting to dress up. I bought myself a new outfit after Christmas (retail therapy!) and wore it once but felt 'wrong' as outside I looked good but inside I felt little and insecure. I also, occasionally, wear a short skirt and boots, which I know Alan likes me in. I had put the skirt on the other Sunday but felt wrong, so changed for trousers. I decided to think why it felt wrong and came up with the answer that I used to dress (not every week but a lot of times) in what I thought the women would admire me in, for my slim figure (which is a laugh, as I would spend the whole time with my tummy pulled in tight thinking I was fat – which I am...) and which men might find me attractive in and so I would be popular and liked (which goes back to my schooldays when I had no friends and so tried to find ways to be liked, like handing round sweets to the boys during lessons but I was only popular until the sweets ran out. I had no real friends at school and did not know how to make any. I was always last to be picked for a team and was picked on and bullied at times. This went on through the time I did my training for teaching horse riding. I spent twelve months as a working pupil and was teased and bullied throughout – all this I had forgotten about).

I decided that there's no point 'dressing the window, if there's nothing in the shop' and that I should be comfortable wearing what I wear for me and no-one else and to grow from the inside.

It is a big thing for me to write about that, as it was to share it with Alan, and one day I shall read this and laugh – and look how far God has bought me in His wonderful care and grace. But this is where I am now, coping with the loss of Tom, living in a new home and work situation and trying to find me and like who I find.

We went to see James in Aberystwyth. We decided to visit him as he is struggling, with Tom but also with going back to Uni. Its the second term – after Christmas – quite common for first year students apparently. I just needed to give him a hug.

In a strange way we are glad that he is struggling as he has shown little signs of grieving and sometimes we felt it was because he cared so little for Tom, but we know he loved him. I have sometimes resented him for not showing emotion and I have to tread carefully in what I have said when he has been home. I just wish we could all be honest with each other, instead of trying to be strong for each other and not upset anyone. He is coming home on Friday for the anniversary of Tom's death, which is on Sunday, a day we are dreading, again building it into something monstrous. It is hard to think of Tom at the moment without tears, thinking of how he was feeling in the week before he took his life and how we did not know or how he felt or what he was thinking. You cannot help but go over it all in your mind. I try to keep busy so as not to think, but the thoughts pop into my mind when I don't expect them and it hurts.

Sunday 30th January 2005

The First Anniversary of Tom's Death

Well, the monstrous day dawned and, as always happened, wasn't nearly as bad as we feared. We fetched Susan and Molly from the airport in the morning after we had put some flowers on Tom's garden – it's funny but I still don't know what to call it – where Tom's ashes are buried – I think I am still in denial really – still not facing that final bit.

James came home, in the afternoon, and we passed the time lost in our own thoughts and memories, each struggling to do what had to be done. At 5:30pm Alan broke down and cried and all the feelings of a year ago came back to him, along with the guilt. What if he had told Tom he was coming to pick me up, instead of just going (as he often did) – he might have been able to stop him. I told Alan that Tom was going to do what he did anyway – he would have waited until Alan went – and that Alan was privileged to have been the last person to see Tom. I would have given anything for that, although Alan doesn't see that, as he moaned at Tom for not finishing the dogs off properly, so that brings its own regrets.

Friday evening we popped over to visit Mum and Dad, to see how they were. We had a pleasant enough time but I came away feeling really frustrated that nobody talked about Tom. I felt a real need to talk about HIM, not what he'd done and how we'd all coped or how he had felt before but to talk about the good times and about what a special person he was and what he meant to each of us. I know we would have cried at the memories but that would have been alright. I just needed to remember.

Saturday was a strange day. The Coffee Room was open so we were involved in that but I could not cope at all and just felt that we should go to Chipping Campden – like I needed to run away, to keep running until I couldn't run anymore. I felt really panicky and the more customers that came in the worse I felt. So after lunch we went with James and walked the hills around Campden. It was enough to be in the fresh air and to talk and find out where James was at. I would have liked to have spent some time just sitting in the church but I didn't suggest it as I didn't think Alan or James would have wanted to (but I didn't ask them, perhaps I should have…).

Sunday, we just got up, as usual, and went to church. Where else would we go; to whom else would we run…? Mum and Dad came to support us. We had a difficult time in the days before, as Mum invited us for lunch, which we declined but couldn't explain why. Again, we just felt that, on the day, we wouldn't know how we would feel until it happened and that we needed freedom to do and be what was right for us and the offer of lunch, which normally would be a good thing, seemed to send us into total panic. A few days later Philip and Hermey invited us, saying we needn't decide until 1pm if we weren't sure but it felt like a really safe place to go and we knew we could be ourselves and talk or not, or cry or not, in a safe environment. How do you explain that to your parents without hurting them? We accepted Phil and Hermey's offer straight away and then Mum asked us again, which tied me in knots as I didn't want to hurt her by saying we had accepted another offer. It was all so difficult at such a difficult time.

Alan insisted we were doing the right thing and that we could still end up coming straight home after the service if that felt right but I was so uncomfortable with the whole issue – and it was just over a meal! I was trying to see it from my parents' perspective and that they were hurting too and just wanted to support us.

Philip asked us if there was a special song that we might like during the service – he probably knew the answer already but we said *My Jesus, My Saviour* which was Tom and Alan's baptism song and both their favourites. Phil said the church would pray for us. I felt very strongly that all the praise and glory be given to God for bringing us through this year. So many people still come up and say that we're strong and an inspiration to them, which is great, but we're not strong. We are weak and we still hurt so much and it is only through the love and grace of Jesus that we are still hanging in there (no pun intended!).

I don't know why I felt so strongly but I just felt desperate that the church should know that God has held us and is still holding us, still bringing us through the valley, that He is real. I am so grateful to Phil that he heard me. We sang the song and it was beautiful and we both had a picture of Tom in Heaven singing his heart out to His Jesus, His Saviour and being in perfect peace; and we were blessed by that. As the congregation was still standing, Phil prayed for us and his prayers were perfect; and God was glorified so wonderfully.

After the service I worried that we were doing the wrong thing by not lunching with Mum and Dad but we had a good lunch with Philip and Hermey and were able to relax and be ourselves and let the pressures melt away; so I knew it was right.

We called in to see Mum and Dad in the afternoon, which was nice, but still no-one talked about Tom. We talked about the service and people in church and the dogs and the weather but we didn't talk about the one person who we should have talked about. I felt really frustrated about that – that nobody talks about him unless we do. He was here for sixteen years and we all wish he was still here but nobody talks about him; maybe it's still too raw. I don't know – maybe that's part of the grieving process to feel as I do now. I wish I could think and remember all the happy times but really I just seem to remember all the times when he was naughty or unhappy – is that normal?

After the evening service, we came home and checked our e-mails and a friend from church had posted something on a blog page called, *Remembering Tom*. It was lovely, and said just what I needed to hear from someone else about our lovely son – the Lord's provision again and in His perfect timing. Thank you so much Jo. I would like to reprint it here so that you might catch a glimpse of what a special person Tom was seen through someone else's eyes.

"A year ago today, the sixteen-year old son of a family we know took his own life. Tom was a remarkable boy – the last kid in the world who you would expect to do such a thing. He always reminded me of Bambi – long legs and great big brown eyes and a beautiful smile. And he was always smiling – he seemed (to me, knowing the family reasonably well but not very closely) to be nothing like those stereotypical moody teenagers. He was pleasant, thoughtful, kind and a pleasure to spend time with. But the most amazing thing about him was his sensitive and observant spirit, expressed in the most beautiful, mature and insightful writing you would expect from anybody, let alone a young boy. I had the privilege of reading some of his poems, and was always touched and impressed by them. In the end,

maybe that sensitive spirit was his undoing. I don't know. I know that, with a history of depression myself, I have feared knowing too much about the thoughts and feelings that led him to such a drastic step, although if I had asked his parents, I think they may have shared that information with me. I have in the past wrestled with such feelings and don't want to go there again.

But the other thing I know is that Tom knew Jesus, and he is now in an incredible place, with all his turmoil and pain long forgotten, and the eternal glory and joy of his Father God filling him. We will see him again, just like we will see our own son Benjamin, and all will be well.

Till then, Tom, I miss you, I remember you with love, and I am praying for your parents Alan and Jackie, and your brother James. God bless..."

It is now nearly the end of February and I only intended for this journal to last a year. Actually, when I started it, I thought I was only going to cover the first week and it would be for our own personal use only. There is so much more to say but for now: there is a tenant in our house in Bidford, we are working together with Susan and Molly as a team after a difficult time on their return from holiday, which was a combination of a lot of things – our low confidence and state of mind which Satan used to blow everything right out of proportion and which we just did not recognise. I didn't think we had taken our eyes off Jesus but I guess we must have and Satan is very clever. But we have all learnt from that time, from when things came to a head – and Alan and I very nearly moved out and went to live in the vacant house in Bidford – but we have become stronger for the experience.

So, to sum up: What have we learned? To trust our Heavenly Father, who loves us with such an amazing, unconditional and complete love, who cares for us and wants the best for us, who hurts with us when we hurt, who gave His only son, Jesus, to walk among us and teach us how to live and love, and who chose to die in agony on a cross so that He could defeat death and sin, and show us the way to eternal life with Him.

We know Heaven is real. We have seen glimpses of it through this year. We know Tom is there. We know he is at peace and we know we shall see him again. It all still hurts, some days more than others. We still don't understand how we can both go for days or weeks without feeling sad and then, just out of the blue, we feel the pain of it all. At the same time, we don't 'start each other off' or set out to feel that way but it just happens. Weird!

I still get emotional in church, especially during prayer times, whether it is for me or not! A special person – not from our church – shared one day that he felt God was saying to us that He still wanted to carry us, that we shouldn't try to do things in our own strength but that we should let Him carry us in all things. I know I have tried to do things in my own strength, especially since we moved to The Riverside Christian Centre. I am very independent and stubborn by nature and that has been my downfall. I suppose I thought that we should move on and put last year behind us and that we couldn't expect God to carry us, that we should be able to stand on our own two feet now, that He had carried us through the valley and set us down on the other side and that it was up to us now – sort of, "Off you go now, you can do it!" But in His wonderful grace He knows we still need Him so much more than we think we do.

I am feeling stronger. I am more aware of myself and the times when Satan can cause me to despair and I can pray against it. I have so much to learn and I want to learn. There is still a lot of baggage that needs to be dealt with but I am not brave enough just yet. My self-confidence is returning, slowly. We have had two successful weekends with group bookings so that all helps but it also takes little to knock me back. But I know God is my strength and He will complete the work He has started in me.

Sometimes I would give anything to be able to turn the clock back; to have a second chance, to be the mother I should have been instead of the mother I was, to spend more time with the boys instead of giving my time to others and doing selfish things like going to the gym. But however bad a mother I was, both James and Tom are sons to be proud of and I love them both and thank God for them.

Little Brown Duck

The little brown duck looked so serene,
As she glided along on a sea of green.
But deep beneath, way out of sight,
She paddled like crazy, with all of her might.
And all who saw her thought she looked fine,
While slowly but surely she went out of her mind.

She knew her place was there on the pond,
With the other ducks, of whom she was fond,
But sometimes it seemed like the worst place to be,
Caught in a spiral of dark misery,
Should she go this way – where to go next?
In rising panic, more and more vexed.

Still on the surface, looking so calm,
Not wanting to frighten or raise the alarm,
She'd swim with the other ducks, quack now and then,
The fear would leave – then come back again,
Each time it did, it was worse than before –
She had to do something, of that she was sure.

But who could she turn to, who could she trust,
Who would be caring, gentle and just?
Who had the answers she needed to hear?
Who had the arms to catch all her tears?
Only one person had that much love,
Her wonderful Father in heaven above.

So she poured out her heart, told Him just how she felt,
He listened intently, gave His hand to be held,
Told her very gently, with words full of grace,
"I can only help you, when you look to my face"
So now on that pond of deep blue and green,
Is a little brown duck, safe and serene.

Jackie   18. April 2005

Run To You

Where can I run to, where can I go,
When everything inside is screaming out 'Nooooo!'
The things you are asking, I think that I can't,
I simply can't do them, or be what you want.
I just want to run, as far as I can,
To hide in a dark place – that can't be Your plan.
I give You my heart, please heal and restore,
Collect all my tears Lord – how many more?
It's hard to sing when you can't see the words,
With your eyes overflowing – you feel so absurd.
It's been such a long time, but the hurt is so raw,
I should be much better, not cut to the core.
So much is going on in my mind –
Struggles and turmoil, it all makes me blind
To Your wonderful love, Your amazing grace,
Revealed afresh when I look to Your face.
I want to serve You, give You my best,
Be filled with Your Spirit, in Your presence to rest,
To know You and love You for all of my days,
To worship completely, lost in Your praise,
To know that the things I do in Your name,
Will bless You and honour You, bring glory and fame.
So it's to You that I'll run, each time I'm afraid,
You'll always be here, that promise You've made,
You'll never forsake me, or turn me away –
Thank you, dear Father, by Your side I will stay.

Jackie. 18. April 2005

Praise You

Praise You that You hold us
Through all the ups and downs,
Your strength and grace are all we need,
Your love for us abounds.

Praise You that when we go our own way;
When we forget You're even there,
Your arms are stretched open and wide
To show us how much You care.

Praise You that You mould us
To become who You need us to be,
That You take and break and remind us
Of our place in eternity.

Praise you that You guide us
By Your word and with Your peace,
Through the power of Your Holy Spirit
You bring us to our knees.

Praise You that then and only then
Will our hearts be in tune with Yours
Our songs, a sacrifice of praise,
Our faithfulness restored.

Praise You that when we're deaf and blind,
You open our ears and eyes to see,
The wonder of Your amazing love,
The beauty of Your majesty.

Praise You that when we're hurting,
When all we feel is pain,
You hold us close, safe in Your arms
'Til we're able to stand again.

Praise you that we have a future
That's awesome, boundless and free,
Because of Jesus' sacrificial love
We can share eternity.

Praise You that when we get there,
We'll meet You face to face,
We'll give You thanks and worship You,
Saved by Your wonderful grace.

Jackie. 21. July 2005

<u>Amazing Love</u>

You pick us up and hold us
In the palm of Your mighty hand.
You carry us always with You,
When life doesn't go the way we've planned.
When upside down is right-side up
And inside is definitely out.
Your arms are there open and wide –
You know what it's all about.
You've loved us since you made us,
You've been here right from the start.
You made us each to worship you –
You put <u>You</u> in our hearts.
And when we don't acknowledge You,
Omit You from our lives,
Still You're watching over us
To see how we each survive.
And when we turn from our evil ways
Give our lives at last to You,
You welcome us as long lost heirs –
And all of heaven rejoices too!
You clothe us and equip us
For the battle that lies in store,
For now that Satan's lost us,
He wants us even more.
And when we walk our painful paths
Through the valley's deep and wide,
We know You're there – we hear Your staff
Gently tapping the canyon side.
We know we can trust You for all things,
Through your grace we will be restored.
We give You thanks and praise Your name,
Our Saviour, Jesus, Lord.
And when we meet in glory
Only then will we understand –
How You could so deeply love us
That You hold us in Your hand.

Jackie. 21. July 2005

September 2005

Well, here we are at the end of September 2005 – feels like a million miles from where we thought we'd be this time last year when we were full of hope and excitement about where God was taking us. At that time we had no concept of our time at The Riverside Christian Centre being for a season only. We were looking much further ahead than that – maybe too far ahead – maybe we were caught up in thoughts and visions of what we could make the place when we took over, so we didn't fully understand, in our naivety, what we should be concentrating and focusing on.

I felt I had watched and learnt an awful lot of what went on and how things were done, when I helped out over the previous summer before we moved in, especially from a 'hands on' practical way. I worked so hard when I was there and so did Alan when he was able. We catered for groups, cleaned up when they'd gone, made all the cakes and biscuits etc, kept it all clean and cobweb free, in fact most of what we did once we'd moved in.

In the scheme of things there didn't seem to be much more that we weren't already doing except that as volunteers we were guided as to what needed to be done, who needed to be where and when. Once we moved in all that stopped. So we did what was required as per our job description and what we felt confident doing but whether that was enough or not, we weren't told. As trainee managers we weren't being trained.

I suppose we were in a fragile state of mind and so we possibly weren't pushed at all but we would have benefited from a more positive approach rather than being left to work it out for ourselves. Naturally, given my already fragile state, this chipped away at my confidence daily.

In March we went to Israel with the church – about thirty of us – a really fantastic time – awesome to see all the places from the Bible and Galilee was just so special. We sailed on a wooden boat across the lake and halfway across they cut the engine and we just drifted. It was a gorgeous day and we just sang and prayed and sat in God's presence –

Someone said the rocking of the boat was like being rocked in Jesus' arms; it was just so amazing. No one wanted to come home; we all felt so at ease there in that country – considering it was at the top of the governments list of places not safe to visit!

Back to The Riverside and things continued to go downhill, for me especially. I felt further from God, was unable to make time to pray except for the times set aside for prayer, which were Riverside focussed or structured. I found my only 'me' prayers were, 'God help me now, I can't do this on my own, I need you' prayers. I was unable to spend time praising Him or even thanking Him. Some of my prayers were, "Make him stop, make him go to sleep." I was very low and had not wanted sex for a long time – probably since January. Alan was very good and understanding and patient but still a man with needs! I think a lot of it was living in the house – and thinking of Susan downstairs! But even when she was across the yard in the office, it was still too close.

In April, I wrote the two poems, *Little Brown Duck,* obviously about myself, and *Run to You,* which was about the problems in the bedroom but also about where I was at the time. I felt I had no-one to share the situation with and I certainly couldn't talk about something so personal and private so I tried to deal with it on my own and with God.

For my birthday at the end of April, Alan arranged for time away on Exmoor. We had a wonderful time! God's hand was upon everything; we walked; we rode and we ate! But we slept in separate beds! My excuse was that the mattress was like sleeping on pebbles! The single bed wasn't a lot better either and I'm sure Alan had hoped for a return to 'normality' while we were away and he was very disappointed. But it was a time of healing (there had been a healing meeting the night before we went away and Phil had prayed for us both). To be able to ride was a real blessing and always sets me free. We saw deer in the woods and on the moors and had fun jumping logs and galloping over open heath land. We got lost – but found amazing scenery that we'd not seen before it was just wonderful!

So we returned home revived and refreshed but still with a long way to go. The church weekend away was held in the middle of May, again with Rob and Marion White, this time talking through the book of Ruth and doubt/faith. We both had a tough 'Tom' weekend. I suppose seeing families together and with all the Riverside baggage, we were quite emotional. I felt panicky about going back there; I really didn't want to. We shared with Rob and Marion how things were for us there and they advised us to put a date on things, a kind of date that we wanted things sorted by and lift it to God and leave it with Him.

On the Saturday night party, at the end we were each given a piece of paper with 'you are a beautiful human person' on one side. We were to stick these on our backs and armed with felt pens set loose to write encouragements on each other's papers. It was awesome what people wrote on ours; how they see us, the way we've done what we've done and coped since Tom died – extremely humbling and really unbelievable – the only one I really believed was the 'nice legs'. (They are my best feature!!)

On Sunday morning we held communion in family groups, which was tough. James was with us and we were part of two or three other families but I was so conscious that there should have been four of us. I had a panic and was crying and just needed to run away. So Alan and I went for a walk up the lane. As we were talking things through I realised that it was just a trick of Satan to keep us away from hearing Rob and Marion so we went straight back to the session.

On the 17th May I started a daily journal. I knew I needed to write things down, how I felt etc, but on a daily basis. Parts of that first entry follow here… *"I know its been a horrible year so far. Its been full of pain and doubt, not just the pain of grief, but so much more, so much unbelief in myself and whether we are doing the right thing in the right place, whether we're really where God wants us, whether I can do everything here I'm supposed to – whether I want to…" "…Don't know how much longer we can live where we are living (in the house) …Steve and Jane have just left with Amy – want to go with them…"* Steve and Jane had been working at the Riverside before we arrived there. They are a lovely couple but unbeknown to us, they too were struggling with being there. They told us later that if they had had the chance, before we agreed to move in, they would have advised us not to…

It was so good to be able to write things down – good and bad, to look back and see what I _had_ achieved when I felt like I wasn't achieving anything. I was keeping things like the menus away from Susan until the last moments because she would change things around or take things off, never encouraging me by saying, "It's good but it might be better to do this or that…" And living in the house was so stressful. Whenever I needed the washing machine it was always full of unwashed clothes, as it was used as a laundry bin. I felt I couldn't take the things out and leave them on the floor, do my one or two loads, and then put the dirty stuff back, as the machine was kept in an under stairs cupboard in the hallway. It would have been obvious what I was doing and I felt it would have looked bad on my part so I ended up doing what was in the machine first, including tumble drying and folding. As often as possible I would try to do our washing first thing in the morning but even then the machine wasn't always empty.

I also found that I ended up cooking for the four of us most evenings and had to plan what we would eat – not easy as Susan and Molly had different tastes to Alan and I. At the end of a long and tiring day I was always asked, "What's for supper?" and had to come up with something quick and tasty that would please all of us; I don't remember that being in the job description! But if I didn't do it, it would usually be fish and chips from town. It got so bad that we would do anything to try to avoid being around at supper time – go to the gym (avoiding the, "What do you want to do that for, haven't you had enough exercise running around here all day,") – bringing its own guilt thoughts that perhaps you should have done more, even though you'd done more than enough! – or visiting friends, or eating what the groups ate. Another diary entry "…have avoided supper for a whole week…I just can't do it… I'm dreading when James comes home (for the summer). How can he feel settled when we are so unsettled…?"

At the May 'healing' meeting, Phil felt led to Revelation 2v17 "_He, who has an ear, let him hear what the Spirit says to the churches. To him who overcomes,_

I will give some of the hidden manna. I will also give him a white stone with a new name written on it, known only to him who receives it" but he did not know why. He felt that he should anoint each person and as he prayed over them, that they should imagine Jesus asking them "What would you like Me to do for you?" It was a special time – total quiet – as Phil went round the room. I asked Jesus to give me His peace, about everything: The Riverside Centre, the past, the future, *everything*, that I would know I was doing His will and where I was supposed to be. As Phil prayed I was filled with peace and felt very calm, which I hadn't felt for a long time.

That peace and calm lasted for about six weeks. I felt more confident in myself, closer to God and able to cope with all at the Riverside. I think I realised for the first time that God loved *me*. I knew for certain in a way that I could put into words that I was loved and forgiven and that I couldn't make God love me any more or less because His love is unfailing, unconditional and new every morning. I understood it all in a different way, I just *knew*. As Rob says, "You know in your *knower*!"

During that time we moved out of the house and into the mobile home, vacated by Steve and Jane. We had to agree for Alan to undertake 'restoration' (building and roofing – not his cup of tea!) work as apparently that is the terms of the mobile home being allowed on site by the planners and also we had had to ask to move into it. It wasn't a natural suggestion but, anyway, it solved all the washing machine and supper problems and gave us our own space and somewhere to retreat to so we were very happy! James was able to come home from Uni. and move into what had been our bedroom in the house, which he was happy with. Things got back to normal for Alan and me in the bedroom for a while and life was good – but it didn't last!

I found I was thinking about Tom a lot more but I felt uneasy and didn't know why. I have written in my diary that I wanted to re-read his letters and things and to watch the Thanksgiving Service again but felt uneasy about doing it – maybe I didn't want to re-open old wounds. I was scared to go back there, scared of letting myself go emotionally, perhaps. I thought it was all dealt with and overcome but it was a strange few weeks. Alan too, was thinking more about Tom, not always good thoughts but we rarely discussed them with each other so didn't know what the other was going through. This was the pattern with The Riverside work too. I suppose we were so busy doing what needed to be done and coping in our own ways that we didn't see what was in front of our eyes. I was only really comfortable when baking or when groups were in or after they'd left because I knew exactly what had to be done and the time scale I had to do it in. I really struggled on Tuesdays and Wednesdays when Alan was out driving and usually I needed him to suggest jobs or to say that what I had planned was good. The other days were better because we worked together and I could lean on him.

I wasn't conscious of negative thoughts – I was still feeling good and praising God for the peace I felt but at the end of June things began to change. An entry from my diary 26th June – *"Really strange feelings at church tonight, I was asked to do the reading, normally I am fine with that and enjoy it but tonight I felt I couldn't do it; I asked Helen to pray for me and during the worship I just wanted to run out – not because of the reading but I was just in a panic! Songs got to me as well and I ended up with tears streaming, praying and asking for God's help and strength to be able to read – anyway I did it, almost stopped halfway through, but praise God, He helped me through…feel weird now though, tired, but also 'odd' want to believe I still have peace but just now its hard to…"*

The following weeks were good and I was back in control and for the July 'healing' meeting Phil asked me to share how I was feeling. I had not told him for a long time about how I'd felt since the meeting but decided that it was time to tell him – more as an encouragement for him. I had my own 'white stone' which Tom had picked up and bought back from Skiathos on our last family holiday along with some driftwood and which I put on display in the sideboard to remind me of God's love for me.

The day of the meeting was not a good day. I was feeling wobbly and negative – about all the work that needed to be done and the lack of staff but I had promised God that I would never refuse an opportunity to praise Him in public and so when Phil asked me I said, "Yes" but also admitted that it was a bad day.

It really hurt to share at the meeting. I felt I did a bad job. I know I was among friends but still felt small and weak. I hadn't written anything down and I always get tongue-tied when I have to speak without notes so I'm not sure I said the right things that I wanted to say and I didn't want to admit where I was emotionally or remember how low I had felt because it was painful. I wrote in my diary:

"…praise God I did it, it means facing it and admitting it, but I am not still living it – God has delivered me through it.

I shared that I found it really tough to praise Him, but that because I promised Him on New Years Eve, I did and have praised Him, even when all I have wanted to do was run away, when everything inside was screaming 'no'; 'you don't mean it',' I can't do it, I'm not worth it etc. but because of that meeting last month and the white stone – I know I am loved, forgiven, precious and so worthy of Jesus' love that He died for me. I know it, deep in my heart, and even when it was hard to pray this morning, I knew God was with me because He promises never to leave me or forsake me.

So many people need to hear that for themselves. Feel peaceful again – still want to cry!"

July was a busy month at The Riverside and I felt very overwhelmed with all that I needed to organise – there were two weekends with big residential and day groups, also the Coffee Room to run and also a birthday party for forty people – and basically three staff! I was nervous of giving Susan menus to look at because she would still change them. I was so nervous that I made mistakes anyway! Alan and I both felt that we should be trusted with menus and food planning as we are good at it and capable of doing a good job but that wasn't the case.

We felt we had to fight to produce what we knew was a right choice, for example, an afternoon tea with sandwiches and not just cake! (We were saved on that one because the group put on their booking form that that was what they were expecting but it was still a battle and we were not able to use quality bread. It had to be thin 'plastic' bread. We realise that cost plays a very important part but that did not come into the argument. Thin, tasteless bread is what you make sandwiches with and that's that!)

A group came whose final numbers were different from the numbers I had taken from the diary – which had been confirmed two weeks prior to arrival and were taken as final figures. Susan had not informed me of the changes and so there was some frantic running around before Friday's supper. I wrote in my diary that I felt useless and just wanted to keep busy. I hadn't been sleeping very well. Another entry; *"…anyway, need to go and work and pray – work to run away from these thoughts – actually they're more like feelings that put me on edge, like a flight reflex, I can't relax, I need to pray for God's peace to return. Am stressed about the afternoon tea, shouldn't be – it's a piece of cake really!! But I don't like it and it scares me."*

Things got worse over the next week – panicky – needing to keep busy – which was good because there was a lot to do – feeling worthless and that I was the one with the problem. I felt that if I wasn't around everything would be alright. I even had Alan married off to someone else in my mind! It was so clear and logical. He and James would get over me and move on and have a much better life without me and she would be a far better mother to James than I had ever been. I knew exactly how and where I would end things, just not when.

I continued to work. We had the big residential group – who messed us about something terrible all weekend – and a day group, and also the Junior Church Camp over. So there was a lot of preparation needed and equipment moving. So everyone had all they needed, in the different places, a stressful weekend under normal circumstances. I lost it on the Friday! Alan got cross with me. He was 'stuck in the middle' as Susan and I were barely communicating by this time. I couldn't face her as I was convinced everything I'd done was wrong or not good enough. I would make a good practical decision about something, but because it wasn't how things were 'done' it was questioned in a critical manner, which just confirmed to me that I was rubbish. I wasn't, of course, but that's how I felt.

The weekend was a success. Everyone was fed and watered and catered for in every way. I had spent much of the weekend in a panic, needing to keep busy and to run away – which Alan didn't really understand, but then neither did I.

I had a difficult time at the Sunday evening service. I was operating the sound desk and feeling 'small'. There was a buzz on the line somewhere and I couldn't work out where it was coming from or how to get rid of it. It didn't seem to bother the congregation but to me it was really loud and served to show me how useless I was because I couldn't stop it. I ended up in tears – Alan was leading the worship and for the final song he threw in, *The Lord's my Shepherd,'* which gets me every time! I couldn't face anyone after the service so tried to hide in the kitchen and the loo but people kept coming in, and in the end I had to go back into the church.

Alan could see I was upset and so we left without saying goodbye to anyone – most unlike us. I was unable to talk to Alan and didn't want anything to eat which made him cross and me feel worse. He wanted to stay home with me the next day, (he had swapped his driving day because of an afternoon tea group coming on the following Thursday) but I insisted I'd be alright and so he went to work.

Monday 18th July 2005

I set my alarm and started work at 8:30am as I had a lot to do. I was in a bit of a state and as I worked the worse I felt and the more I seemed to panic. I did not want to see anyone – or for anyone to see me – did not want to go downstairs for the worship time so kept busy doing anything I could on the top floor – as far away from anyone that I could get, sorting out beds, making sure they looked nice and setting up two rooms for separate ladies on retreat days. I just worked hard and fast and all the time feeling worthless, useless and stupid.

Susan called me to say there was a visitor for me so I had to go downstairs. I tried to compose myself and to smile at Susan but it didn't really work. The visitor was Philip who was worried about us because of our hasty departure from church. He said he had come for a chat. I didn't know where to go to talk. I couldn't make a decision, didn't want to talk, wanted to keep busy etc. But anyway we went to the mobile home. I don't think I made much sense. I could only talk a few words at a time and mostly about needing to be busy, getting back to work. I had too much to do but I was fine. I would be okay.

Philip told me I wasn't fine. I was ill and I needed to see a doctor. He offered to drive me to see my G.P. but I said I would ring after he had gone. I couldn't keep still. I was still very agitated about needing to be busy and in a way I felt trapped by Phil because by being there he was stopping me from working and that was wrong. But he was very patient with me and asked me questions that I answered as best as I could. I said I felt it had been wrong for us to go to the Riverside, that it was all my fault, that I was worthless and everyone would be better off without me. He did not judge me or tell me I was wrong, just how much God loved me and how precious I am to Him. He prayed for me and then let me go back to work as he could see I needed to.

I felt that I just wanted to cry and never stop but I continued to work (and fought the tears). I worked in the Coffee Room, serving customers and washing up and in between cleaning all the shelves and doing anything to be busy. I didn't phone the doctor – I wasn't brave enough and I didn't know what to say.

By the time I had finished work and fed the dogs it was half past six, which was when Alan got home. I cooked him a meal but didn't eat anything myself – hadn't eaten all day but I wasn't hungry. He was cross with me because I wouldn't eat but he was also cross with himself because he didn't know what to do or say to me. Philip rang and spoke to Alan but I don't know what they said as Alan took the call in the bedroom. He did say that Phil had told him he had to talk with me. Phil spoke to me and asked if I had phoned the doctor. I said I had been too busy but that I would see him the next day.

Alan and I went for a walk in the evening and were finally honest with each other – probably for the first time in ages. I was able to tell Alan all the awful thoughts I was having, about wanting to take my life. It wasn't because of what Tom did or wanting to be with him but it was because I just felt everyone would benefit if I wasn't around. We also talked honestly about The Riverside and our future there and discovered that neither of us was happy or that it was where we wanted to be.

Alan hadn't told me how he felt because he could see I was struggling with everything and he just made the best of each situation and got on with things. But he felt increasingly over the months that our time there was for a season and not for life as we had thought when we had gone there. It was so good to be honest. Why hadn't we done it a long time ago instead of burying our heads?

Alan tried to get me an appointment with the doctor but couldn't get one until the Wednesday. I was very surprised however to get a phone call from the doctor asking how I was and saying he was sorry he wasn't available that day but if I needed anything or anyone there was a lovely lady locum who would help. Alan said later that when he phoned the surgery he had said that he had already lost one son and wasn't prepared to lose his wife as well!

He stayed home with me and told me I didn't need to go to work, which I was feeling very guilty about, even though the thought of going filled me with horror. So I cleaned the mobile home from top to bottom and rested only when Alan told me to!

I saw the doctor the next day, felt very nervous and weepy having to admit how I was feeling, but he had been expecting something like this since Tom died and knowing what our plans were in selling the house and moving to The Riverside. He was very gentle, caring and persuasive and told me I would have to trust him on this one and take the happy pills that I'd been fighting for so long. He also said we would benefit from counselling. I felt so guilty about taking the tablets I felt I had let God down but I did agree to take them and to see him again in a week's time.

I felt I needed to talk things through with Philip so we went straight to Campden. He was brilliant again and listened and waited while I cried and he said that I was not letting God down at all. I was having such an internal battle about the tablets but it was funny as when I 'gave in' and said I would take the first one, Alan said he'd go and get them from the car while Phil offered to fetch me some water – talk about making sure I wouldn't change my mind!! I declined their offers and waited until we got home, but it was still really hard for me to take the first one.

While we were with Philip, we shared about The Riverside and what it was like. We'd give it until November; our own coffee shop was still very much on our hearts and back on our agenda. It was good to be able to share and put Phil in the picture as we hadn't really told him before what it was really like and the difficulties we faced. He was aware that there were difficulties and that people (staff and volunteers) didn't seem to stay long but he didn't know why. He suspected, but didn't know.

It seems to me that whole, strong people went in to serve the Lord in that place but broken people came out. Yes, visitor's lives were touched and people met with God there but as for the workforce it was a different story. (I only know this with the benefit of hindsight and speaking to those who have experienced it). We concluded that we needed to be honest and brave and confront Susan and Molly to get things sorted once and for all.

We had shared our frustrations with a couple of people and were asking them to pray specifically for us that we would hear from God about whether he wanted us to stay at The Riverside or to move on and if so where to.

I really could not face work and neither could Alan but he was really staying home to watch over me. It was nice to be told what to do and more importantly, what not to do! Alan covered things with Susan and said I would not be going back to work for a while. The tablets made me feel quite sick and I was very tired despite sleeping really well. I had weird dreams, mostly about Tom. The best thing was that Alan and I were closer than ever – except in bed but even that led to a gentler side of Alan as he discovered how understanding and patient he can be. We were open and honest in all things that we talked about –The Riverside, Tom, our future and our feelings for each other.

Although I was taking the tablets every day, I still felt depressed and seemed to be getting worse not better. I was scared stiff to even go out of the mobile home and avoided people as much as possible. I did do some work in the Centre but it was all cleaning sort of stuff where I could be on my own and just get on with it and run back to the mobile home when I'd had enough.

From my diary; "… *today I feel really scared about going out of the mobile home, want to run away (from what?) Feel like staying in under the duvet all day. Feel useless because I let Alan down again – he wants (needs) to have sex but I just cannot. I don't like his hands all over me, I wish he'd just hold me – but he can't. I just freeze and pray he'll stop, but he doesn't – why can't I just let him, I know I've done that before and I know how it makes me feel afterwards, but he's been so good about everything so that piles more guilt and pressure on me, he says I haven't let him down but I know I have, its constant rejection, I guess, in his eyes.*
Anyway, time to go, take a deep breath and just get out there!…"

The only time I felt really good was after a run or the gym because I knew I had done something positive and I had achieved something for myself. I was also dieting during this time and being in control of what I ate was really good. I had started 'healthy eating' at the end of June when we moved into the mobile home and I was cooking just for the two of us but it was good to lose the weight and be in control as I felt so helpless otherwise.

We didn't get to discuss things with Susan and Molly until the first of August. It was a very difficult meeting and both sides had disappointments with the other but we started and finished with prayer and we were honest with each other. Both Susan and Molly were on the defensive and I would rather have been anywhere else but I promised Alan that I would let him do the talking and so he did. We tried to be positive and we admitted that we weren't perfect and we'd probably done a lot of things wrong. Susan was disappointed that we hadn't asked questions. We didn't ask what sort of questions we should have asked.

We felt, as I said before, that we had learnt a huge amount last year before we moved in, (but all of that seemed to have been forgotten and was never mentioned). We were capable of continuing to do the same things, and Susan would show us what else we needed to learn as we went along. Anyway we hugged and left, both Alan and I feeling that we had not been heard and that nothing would change.

August was a very quiet month so Susan and Molly went away for the second week and agreed that we could have the next two weeks off, which gave us all some breathing space. During this time we began looking for our own coffee shop and looked at several opportunities in and around Moreton. We felt that we could not stay at The Riverside any longer and that the time was right to start our own venture.

I was 'scared' to even go out of the door and to work in The Riverside building unless it was with Alan but the thought of buying and running our own coffee shop did not faze me in the slightest. It all felt so 'right'. We were increasingly frustrated that we weren't able to be effective in outreach at the Riverside. People who came were already Christians. It was great to provide an atmosphere where they could meet with God and to feed them physically while He ministered to them spiritually but even within the coffee room the majority of those who came, came because they knew it was a Christian place and they were already Christians (and because they could get a cheap meal, as there were no set charges, you were just encouraged to put in a donation, which some people took advantage of). We did not really reach out to those who just passed by and called in and, in any case, felt quite awkward about doing so, as if we had to 'pounce' on them and convert them there and then before they left!

We had a more relaxed week while Susan and Molly were away. I had organised jobs to do which I managed comfortably even while Alan was away driving and we were able to think and talk straight about where we thought our future lay. As they came back on the Sunday evening we did not see them until the morning of our first day's holiday and then only met to cover what we had prepared for the family of seven who were holidaying at The Riverside for a week.

We had initially thought about going away for a few days but it was a big issue to have someone from outside come and live in the mobile home to dog-sit whilst we were gone. (It would have had to have gone before the Trustees etc.) So we decided to stay put and 'holiday at home'. Looking back, it was God's hand on us, as we wouldn't have achieved all that we did if we had gone away.

So we set to work and started to look for somewhere to live and somewhere to work. I insisted I did not want to rush into anything; that we should take our time and think and pray all decisions through.

One place we looked at early on, we had dismissed as being too small. I had, in my mind, a premises big enough to hold a good sized coffee room and also a good sized book/gift shop area but increasingly, as we looked at different places, I realised that they were well out of our price range and also too big to manage on our own. I had not enough knowledge of books to be able to promote and sell them effectively as well as running the coffee shop. The one we had dismissed kept coming back to us. It was small enough for us to manage together, well within our price range, (using the equity of our Bidford house) and the owner wanted a quick sale. We also needed somewhere to live; that we could rent and be allowed to take the dogs; not easy to find as most places (including our own house at Bidford) won't let you take pets.

Well, the first house we looked at in Moreton, is the house we are now settled in and it has an enclosed back yard that we were able to put a shed and run in for the three outside dogs. It was empty and available just when we needed it so we knew it was where God wanted us to move to. It is so good to be back in Moreton. It almost feels like we never left. It is wonderful for the three of us to be under the same roof. I had increasingly needed for that to happen whilst at The Riverside, to be a 'family' again, rather than for James to sleep elsewhere on the premises.

We were grateful to Susan and Molly for accommodating James so well and helping him to feel so welcome but I just needed for him to be under my roof – maybe just part of my insecurity. We all just made the best of everything and every situation for so long at The Riverside and James especially had so much to cope with that year, from losing his brother in that way, to going to university and his parents uprooting and selling the house that really was 'home'. He coped admirably, but said, once we'd moved, that The Riverside never felt like going home, a nice enough place to live but not home. And it must have been difficult for him when he came back to see how we weren't coping, although it improved for a while once we moved into the mobile home.

So anyway, as I write, we are in the process of buying the Tearoom that we said was too small! It is in Stow on the Wold, at the end of an enclosed courtyard and is known as 'The Old Bakery Tea Rooms'. We hope to be in and open for business early in November – and as it's halfway through October now – we are running out of time!

We feel it has God's hand upon it and are praying for it to be a real blessing to Him. I *know* I can do it. It's a frustrating time just now as there is so much going on in our heads to think about and prepare and we just want to get in and start! It is so exciting but also daunting as there is a huge risk if it all goes wrong. Have we got it wrong and have we heard properly, and is it what we should be doing. I still want to hear God say, "Yes, it is here, dummy!" But, I trust it to be right because I just know I can do it and I have a peace about it that I never felt at The Riverside. I think I just went along with what everyone else thought and trusted them rather than my own feelings and once the wheels were in motion it was too late to stop them.

But it was not totally wrong to have gone there. If we had not sold our house, we wouldn't have the Bidford house and the equity in that. We wouldn't have been able to clear all those years of debt. We have learnt that we can live and work together and still have fun and we have brought to the attention of those who need to know the problems at The Riverside and why people are unable to stay and work for long and so hopefully things there can move on. We still believe we were the right people for the job and if we had been allowed to, could have made such a difference.

As far as Tom goes, it is a tough time at the moment. I miss him with a physical hurt. I want to hold him and see him and help him, all the things I should have done. It is his eighteenth birthday on the 20th of this month. We want to mark it but don't know how – might buy a tree or something!

We shall probably be at Alpha (where else) on the evening of his birthday and James says he isn't worried about marking it in any way. It is all very strange!

We awarded a prize in his memory at school, which went to a lovely girl. It is, *The Tom Slough Memorial Award* for 'community spirit' in Year 11. We know he would be behind us and supporting us with the tearoom but I would still give anything for him to still be here, for him not to have felt as he did. Sometimes I 'see' him in my mind, when I open the bedroom door and it cuts my heart like a knife to remember, even just to think of him 'out of the blue' when your mind is on something else. It is good I suppose, shows we haven't forgotten him, but I thought all the pain would have been dealt with by now. Our G.P. wants us to have counselling. I haven't managed to sort anything yet, but we will, even if only to be told we are okay and don't need it.

So, that's where we are at and what's happened in the last few months. We feel 'set free' since we left and moved here. People tell me how well I look and generally I feel great. (Just now, I'm really tired all the time and am still on the happy pills. I feel frustrated that when I feel great, in the back of my mind I think it's just the pills and not the real me and I want it to be the real me as I think I know who I am now and I actually like me! So really I want to come off the pills but I will be guided by the doctor).

December 1st 2005

We are on the verge of signing for the teashop, which is both wholly exciting and terrifying at the same time! We have everything we need. It's been 'fun' to choose china, write menus, buy a dishwasher etc and frustrating not being able to have a shop to put them in. It seems to have taken ages but we are assured it hasn't really (three and a half months). I haven't worked, having been a lady of leisure, which has been again both a blessing and a trying time. I am still trying to sort myself out, to find out who I am and why I feel like I do, which means thinking of my growing up, which I find painful, and also remembering things about the boys' childhoods and the way I brought them up.

We have started counselling – we had to! My G.P. was going to beat me with a big stick if we hadn't started counselling by the time I saw him in November! Alan sees a guy and I see a lady. I felt uncomfortable about seeing a man. I was scared enough about the whole process anyway and I feel at ease with my lady, although she drops some very searching questions in at unexpected moments! (In truth, we only attended two or three sessions as we felt they were doing more harm than good – especially in my case; bringing up things that we felt were not relevant to Tom and it wasn't really specifically bereavement counselling – our fault in the people we chose – should have trusted the doctor!!).

Tom's eighteenth was, as always seems, a day that we dreaded and this time we were proved right. Ever since Tom was born we knew we would one day celebrate James' 21st and Tom's 18th in the same year and month, so to not have him here was awful. The pain, as I've mentioned, was much sharper and more 'real' than ever before whenever we thought of him.

We spent the day with James in Aberystwyth for his 21st birthday. He had Uni. commitments. We met him for coffee, shopped for his present – a signet ring, (suggested by Philip!) so that he can wear it always and be reminded of how much we love him and a smart watch to go with his suit that Mum and Dad gave him. We joked that all he needs now is a girl. Then he had a lecture so we wandered round the town and met up for lunch before he had an afternoon's screening to watch. We left at about 2:30pm and he continued the celebrations with his friends during the evening (!!!).

Tom's birthday was on a Thursday and right up to the day itself we didn't know what to do with it. James came home at lunchtime, which I was cross about as I had hoped he would come home the evening before. I got quite worked up as it got later and later before he met us at Campden at 2:00pm. We had eye appointments in Banbury first thing. I hadn't realised it was Tom's birthday when I made the appointments, but we kept them anyway. It was something to do. I wanted to buy a wreath from the market stall that does really nice arrangements but the funfair was in town and the market wasn't there. So we ended up with red roses from Morrison's which actually were nice and lasted a while. But they were not what I wanted....

So we met James and put the flowers on the grave (first time I have written that...) and went for some lunch in Campden. Matt and two others had put white lilies on the grave in the morning. Phil had seen them so told us who it was. It was a lovely thought of them.

Once we got home we should have sat and talked, but we got busy – Alan fixing something on the computer and I had to make an Alpha meal for the course that night, and James sat watching telly. It was a horrible afternoon; I suppose I was still a bit cross with James, although I had said to him that I was disappointed that he hadn't been home earlier. Anyway, because we had Alpha and were taking somebody for their first time, we arranged for James to go to some friends for supper and company, which was just right for him. We picked him up – stayed for a drink first – and so it was 11:30pm when we got home. We felt we should just pray about the day and then share about how we were feeling, which we did and it was a special time. We admitted we hadn't handled it at all well and James shared how he was feeling, at least. He answered my questions as I tried to guess what and how to ask so he could open up.

So that was that! What should have been a day of celebration for Tom reaching eighteen, was a day of pain and emptiness for each of us. I felt we had been 'allowed' to feel more than before, that God hadn't abandoned us but that we needed to feel emotions that we were/are still trying to deny.

Since then, life has been good – frustrating at times but good! We are making the most of lazy mornings in bed, not getting up before 9:00am and relaxing and not feeling bad about it because once we have signed everything on the shop, life won't be the same again!

We have a passion for the shop to be a place where Jesus is the guest at every table, whether people know He is there or not. We want to show Jesus' love in a real way by treating every customer as special – through the atmosphere, service and food and in any way we can. We don't want to 'push' Jesus down their throats but we are not afraid to be seen and to stand out as Christians.

We will have some of my poems on the wall and we want to be ready with answers when people ask about our faith. The biggest thing on our hearts is that we are not in it for the money but to serve God. It has to pay for itself and us. Alan will still drive for two or three days a week but it would be wonderful if he didn't have to, at the end of the day. I believe that God put the 'shop' on my heart when I became a Christian in November 1999. It never even crossed my mind before then but became a burning desire, although I never knew why. He put me in the right places to learn what I needed to learn but I could see no way that we could ever afford it.

Even when we were thinking of buying the teashop in Moreton, we really couldn't see how it could happen with our finances the way they were. It wasn't a burning desire all the time but it never went away. I believe that God has used what Tom did. He never caused Tom to do what he did – that was Tom's own choice – to bring about what was on His heart for us. Maybe if Tom were still here, we would have gone down the teashop route when he had left home and we could have got our finances back on track. Perhaps that was God's plan for us but instead He has used what happened to grow our faith and our love for Him and each other to serve His purpose much sooner.

Will keep you posted....

1st December 2005

I dreamt I was riding – a lovely bay gelding. We were galloping across country, through trees and heather and our spirits were one. I felt free and exhilarated, as I always am on horseback. Nothing compares to that feeling. We were flying over fences, jumping them as they came into our path. I remember the feeling of rising and landing as one. There was no communication – he wanted to jump and I wanted to go with him. I trusted him. It was a sunny day. The wind was in my hair and it was fantastic, even when I got a bit 'left behind' at one jump – he jumped bigger than I expected but it was great! It was a real and vivid dream.

2nd December 2005

I was praying about the Holy Spirit day – how much I needed it and how much I longed for God to speak to me – to show me what I needed to do – to forgive myself.

As I prayed I remembered the dream and realised that the horse was the Holy Spirit and that that is the relationship between us. I trust in Him and He will run with me; helping me overcome all obstacles, to fly in my relationship with Jesus. I feel this is a new start. The old has gone. I **can** do all things through Jesus Christ, my Lord, who strengthens me.

I will no longer say, "No, I can't," but "Yes I can, and I will."

As a church, we had taken part in a *Freedom in Christ* course led by Philip, which ran over several weeks. The *Holy Spirit Freedom in Christ* day took place on a Saturday and the theme was forgiveness through the power of the Holy Spirit. After the first session we were encouraged to forgive those people who we felt we needed to forgive, which was a powerful time for everyone there.

The second session invited us all to do the hardest thing and to forgive ourselves. This was so amazing for me but <u>so</u> difficult. I remember praying and asking God how to do it and Phil speaking from the front, asking us to say the words, *"I forgive myself."* People, all around, were doing just that and it was very emotional. I remember the sound of gentle weeping from the rows in front and behind but I could not do it. We were encouraged to speak the words out but I could not open my mouth. I was crying and I knew I had to do it, to forgive myself. My eyes were tight shut and I was all screwed up inside and I kept saying, *"I can't."* Maybe I was trying to hold on to the guilt and the pain – punishing myself because I felt responsible for what Tom did because I felt I had been a rubbish mother. If I'd been a better mother maybe he would not have killed himself.

Anyway, every question I asked of God, everything I needed Him to tell me was immediately answered by Phil from the front. It was like it was just me and God in the room. How could Phil know exactly what

I was asking God? I knew I had to respond, to do what God said. I felt totally loved and held in his arms throughout, but it was still something I had to do and I was the only one who could do it. No-one else could say the words for me, even if I wanted them to. I felt Phil willing me from the front to just do it; just say it. I remember Alan, by my side, encouraging me. But the more he did the worse I felt – more rubbish, more guilt. Phil didn't stop speaking. He kept saying, "Forgive yourself. Say the words, 'I forgive myself' gently but forcefully." I felt I must be the only one left to say it and after what seemed a lifetime I did, quietly out loud, amid buckets of tears and with relief from Alan that finally we could move on with the session.

It was such a powerful thing to have done and I am still at peace with myself because of it. I know that God never blamed me for what Tom did. I never once needed His forgiveness. The guilt was all my own and of my own making and would have eaten me up if I had not had the opportunity to forgive myself in that way. If you are holding yourself to ransom, holding on to guilt that you don't need to, then I urge you to find someone who you trust. Share my experience with them and ask them to help you do the same; and to pray with you; but you must speak it out. It will not be so powerful if you just say it in your mind. God will still hear it but *you* won't and it is the speaking it out, saying, "I forgive myself" that is so liberating. Be gentle with yourself and take time if you need to but do it.

There was a break for lunch but I felt I had to go to Tom's grave and spend time there, which I did on my own. It was such a special time and I felt such a peace and release. When we got home I wrote the following piece.

3rd December 2005

Holy Spirit Freedom in Christ Day

Today I have forgiven myself.

I have stood before Tom's grave and told him out loud that I am sorry – for not telling him how much I loved him – for putting other things before him – work, church etc – that I didn't know him – for not being there when he needed me – for not giving him the things that he needed or wanted – for not listening to him – for being a bad mother.

I stood and thanked God for Tom, and said sorry to Him that He created Tom in me and I let him down. Tom was so beautiful and deserved so much more than I ever gave him.

I thanked God for His gift of creative writing – a lasting legacy from Tom.

And I cried.

I have forgiven, in God's presence, all those who teased and bullied me – pupils, teachers and work colleagues throughout my life.

I have forgiven all those who bullied Tom – at St. David's where they didn't take it seriously enough. I have forgiven the boy who strangled Tom on the school bus and maybe put into his mind about hanging, because he blacked out.

But most of all I have forgiven myself.

I have forgiven God – because I trusted Tom to him – but I know I deserve His forgiveness so much more because He first trusted Tom to me.

Help Me Pull Through

I love you Lord and I know that you love me,
But right now, my life seems full of misery,
Things I thought I'd dealt with keep coming back –
It's too easy to say, 'it's just Satan's attack'.
I'm doing my best Father – I'm doing it for you.
But I can't see the point, Lord help me pull through.
I serve with a smile, talk like I care,
Most days I'm O.K. – today I despair.
Keep taking the tablets, perhaps up the dose,
One or two packets…maybe one day – who knows?
You've blessed us so much Lord – a house and the shop,
So many chances to share 'til we drop!'
It hurts each time I hear Alan say – "we didn't know" –
Because I did know, but I didn't let it show,
I was too scared of facing the problems he had,
They were our fault really – his own mum and dad.
So much more we should have been and said,
He might have been here now, instead he is dead.
We buried his ashes – poured him out like dust,
I need to hold him–it just feels like I must.
So I'm doing my best Lord, I'm sharing for you,
Giving you glory, pointing to you,
And each time I give it hurts a bit more,
I don't understand why it should still be this raw,
But I'll give what I can, it's the least I can do –
Maybe one day someone will give their life to you,
Because of something we've shared of the pain that we've known,
And the way that you've carried us, and the way that we've grown
Stronger and stronger – one day at a time,
But I don't feel that strong Lord, – people think that I'm fine,
Sometimes it seems no-one listens, or cares,
There's no-one to love me, or acknowledge I'm there.
I am sure that's how Tom felt, and maybe that's why
He couldn't go on living, he just had to die.
So it really is my fault, I should have done more –
I thought this was dealt with, why's it surfaced once more?
These feelings of guilt are the truth in their way,
They're things I must deal with as I cope every day.
Keep me safe Lord as I live my little life for you,
Please bless me and hold me and help me pull through.

Jackie. 23. July 2006

Jesus and Me

Jesus, what will I see
When I look in Your eyes?
Depths of love and compassion
That none can describe.

Jesus, how will I feel
When I'm in Your embrace?
Will I feel Your power
Yet know Your grace?

Jesus, what will I say
If I'm able to speak?
Thank you – I love You –
Or will I just weep…?

Jesus, what will I hear
When You call my name?
Will my heart melt, and wash away
All trace of hurt and pain?

Jesus, will I believe
When you say You love me?
Will I finally know
And my heart be at peace?

Jesus, of all of these things
I know one thing for sure,
Because of the cross
It's You I adore.

Jackie. 21. May 2007

October 2008

Wow! I have just read that for the first time since I wrote it. Although I have had every intention of updating this journal, I just haven't had the time or inclination. Also, because of the painful memories of The Riverside Christian Centre and our time there, I didn't want to revisit it. But there is always a time for everything and I believe that now is right to finish this – I want the whole 'story' to be completed by the 5th anniversary of his death in 2009.

This was always going to be the hardest part to write as it is really about me and the things I have gone through – and gone through by myself with God holding my hand because I was unable to tell anyone how I felt. But God is amazing as always and has delivered me from all fear. He has set my feet firmly on the rock of His love for me. He has bought me to this point where I feel confident to share myself because I know that if only one other 'hurting' person reads this they will be touched by His love and seek Him for themselves and then for me all the pain will be worth it.

The shop has been open now for almost three years and has been incredibly hard work but really rewarding. Alan gave up driving to be full time in the shop. We chose to make as much as possible home-made (the only things I don't make are bread and pastry), not because I am a fantastic cook (because I'm not) but because that way we can control the quality and we know exactly what is in each food item, when it was made and how good it tastes. Our suppliers are great and everything is fresh and good quality and that is what makes us successful in the earthly realm!!

Most importantly for me, to buy cakes etc in, ready made, is not giving my best and Jesus deserves our very best and all we can be as that's what He gave for us. He didn't just get a little bit beaten and a little bit crucified on the cross and came down when He'd had enough but He gave EVERYTHING, all of Himself for us. So we should at least try to give Him the best of ourselves in return. Also we simply can do no less than we do – we have tried!! It is who we are in Christ and in serving Him. Believe me, we are both really lazy people, given the opportunity. It's just that the shop doesn't give us the chance to be lazy but God does look after us when we need Him to.

God has blessed us with a love of simply feeding people with good food but He has blessed us both with a desire to feed people in a far deeper way and to use our testimony on each table to touch people for Him.

We don't believe in making the shop overtly Christian so there is no cross on the wall but through the testimonies there is a cross on each table! Customers can read the testimony or not, it is their choice. Some people come lots of times before they read it!

Our hearts' desire is for Jesus to be the guest at every table whether He is recognised or not and whether customers come for the first or hundredth time.

We don't focus on the cost but we focus on quality food and service and a comfortable time on every level. Alan is fantastic out front and has some amazing conversations with people and shares some of their heartaches as they open up to him. It is a privilege to be used in that way. Customers think they are only coming in for a coffee but they leave refreshed in a much deeper way.

The menu has been amended over the three years. I used to have so much on it that it was a nightmare trying to keep up with it all. I remember very early on I thought I would do a daily 'special' and I tried it one Saturday. I bust a gut getting everything ready – basically sausage and mash but with extra special sausages, red wine gravy and vegetables etc and not one portion sold. So I thought, *"Ok God, I won't do a special!!"* and that is how it has gone on. God has looked after us so well and the menu now is simple, uncomplicated and has something for every thirst and every need – sound familiar? Isn't that what Christianity is about…?

We have lost count of the number of testimonies we have printed but we know that they go all over the world. I used to get frustrated because we didn't know how they were touching people's lives and what impact if any for God but I have learnt to just trust and know that somehow, somewhere, He will use them, in His timing, for His glory.

We have heard from people who have not visited us but who have been touched by our story because somebody took a testimony for them, to help them in a difficult time.

So, that's the shop three years on – thriving – thanks to God's hand upon it. I should just say, in no way am I looking for free advertising by writing about the shop – we have never advertised. Our customers all come by word of mouth but you know me by now – I just tell it like it is!! Also we try very hard not to be known as a *'Christian Teashop'*. We are simply Christians who run a teashop but we realise that is what we are known as and for and if it raises Jesus' name in the town then it has to be a good thing! But all that telling of God's love has the attention of another who would seek to destroy all that we stand for and has tried a number of ways to do so.

For the whole of our first year, while trying to rebuild my confidence in myself and cope with all that running a new enterprise entailed, I still had suicidal thoughts – still thought I was rubbish and still thought everyone would be better off without me. I was still taking the happy pills and still not able to tell anyone how I felt.

On the shop's first birthday I had the perfect opportunity to end my life and I almost took it. I was under so much stress and pressure, trying to be what everyone wanted and what I thought everyone expected. Outwardly things were really good; shop was good; we had had two holidays abroad – there were good stress-free times for me in that first year – it wasn't all horrid. But towards December 2006 – I suppose between Tom's birthday and Christmas – I just let it all get to me.

I always knew how I would take my life: overdose and alcohol, especially when we were at the Riverside Christian Centre but I never had the two means available at the same time because I had no money of my own or the wherewithal to go out and buy enough quantities to do the job properly. Well on the shop's first birthday I did. We had been invited to a birthday party to celebrate but I was in such a state I refused to go (I was in a far worse mental state than I had been whilst at The Riverside but on the surface I kept it fairly together and did what I had to do to keep the shop going). I insisted that Alan went to the party, although he was insisting that he didn't so he could stay with me, but in the end I won and he went, only because we knew how much trouble our hosts had gone to.

As soon as I had the house to myself I thought I could just get on with it and the voice in my head told me just that. Now was my opportunity! If I really wanted to end it all the pills were in the cupboard and the wine was downstairs.(It is quite worrying actually that we could purchase vast amounts of Paracetamol and Ibuprofen as well as wine from the warehouse that we get all the shop stuff from. There is a limit on how many tablets you can buy from a chemist or supermarket but not from a warehouse. So you can buy a dozen packs of sixteen tablets or more and nobody bats an eyelid. It is wrong!) Anyway, now all the things that I didn't have in place at The Riverside were there in the house. I just had to get them and get on with it.

Except, actually, when push came to shove, I didn't want to get on with it and I told the voice in my head that actually I wanted to live, to serve God, to be with my family. A huge weight left me and I spent the afternoon really peaceful, reading and just enjoying being. I was unable to talk of this for a year, until the shop's second birthday, when I told Alan. It had been so real, so close. I don't know if the voice was God or the devil but I never felt that way again; those thoughts totally left me.

In March 2006, I came off the happy pills and have never looked back. Yes, I have been extremely stressed lots of times but I have not wanted to take my life. Recently though, the thoughts have hovered in the background. and I reach a point where I feel that there is an inevitability that one day I will take my life, when I feel I can't go on but I am at peace with that (it releases the hold over me) and I pray that God will take me first but not until I have done all that I can do for Him and for His glory.

One morning, as soon as I woke up, God said to me, "Sell Bidford," so I said okay and told Alan. Briefly, we put the Bidford house on the market. The tenant quickly found somewhere else in the village and we sold and completed it within a month. This enabled us to pay off the business loan for the shop, which we now own outright.

We moved house on June 7th, to a house which I believe was a fulfilment of the prophecy given before we moved to The Riverside and which everyone assumed was for The Riverside at the time – *"You will find a place prepared for you,"* from Mark's gospel.

It is a three-storey town house, four years old and decorated and furnished (carpets, curtains, light fittings etc) to a much better standard and taste than we could ever have come up with. It has everything I have always wanted – in the kitchen and bathrooms (it has three…one each!), a tidy, small landscaped garden with an awesome pink Clematis along the length of the garden, and I still, after eighteen months, look at things and say – "I've always wanted one of those!!"

The mortgage was a big step and a big decision but the house felt so right and so peaceful that we went for it. The evening that we first got the keys we ended up sitting on the floor, in the living room, eating biscuits and drinking Champagne that the previous owner had left for us – it felt so perfect! There is room for James to have his own space but still be part of the family and we just love it to bits – for the time being! Strangely, we never felt it is a 'forever' house – don't know why but we thank God for it often and for His provision (still do and it's now 2010!).

I found an extract in my diary, dated 30th March 08, and I feel it is appropriate to reproduce it here as it tells how I was and then I can tell how God changed me and answered my prayers.

"Lord I come to you,
Let my heart be changed, renewed,
Flowing from the grace
That I've found in you…

This was the song I chose for my baptism in 2000, six months after asking Jesus into my life. I've often wondered why I chose it (I didn't really know it at the time) but I think God chose it for me and I've used it as a prayer quite often.

Tonight the words jumped off the screen at me. I needed to hear from God how to solve the deep unhappiness within me. I've thought for a while I have to change. I can't go on the way things are, so it's down to me and God's grace to make the changes that are so hard for me.
There is hardly any contact between Alan and myself – the odd intertwining of feet

and I put my hand on his shoulder before I go to sleep (he faces the other way – unless he wants my body, which is my worst nightmare still) but that is all there is and it affects our work life. The last time we held each other was 19th October 07, the night before Tom's birthday and Helen gave us a card with beautiful words. We just wanted him back and for the words to have been unnecessary. I know it's a two way thing and it seems I am the only one trying. Alan has always had a problem calling my name and it has become a huge issue for me. He can call others by their names but I am just 'can you' (come here, do this, fetch that etc).

Something has to change! I have felt this weekend that I cannot be bothered because I have tried before – we have spent time with Phil, me saying the hardest most intimate stuff two years ago, to try and make us more accountable to each other and here we are again – nothing's changed! But, if I don't make the effort, what then? I made my vows before God, even though I didn't know Him. He knew me and the vows were for better or for worse...

So, Father God, I cannot do it without you. Change my heart. Soften it towards Alan. Help me to set the example. Help me and encourage me and give me Your grace. Help me with the physical side. It is the last thing I want to do because of hurts in the past between us – I need to forgive him so much. Please help me with this and to know it is done. Help me to look back at this in six months (30 Sept 08) and to see the changes You have made in us. Lord, You know my heart and my needs as well as my doubts and fears. I love You and I can't do this without You. Make me fall in love with Alan again and him with me and help us to keep you at the heart of our marriage. Amen."

Well those six months have passed and God heard my prayers, although things almost got worse before they got better. I felt we probably should separate, thought that was the only answer – bear in mind this was only between God and me. I felt I could not share how I felt with anyone, for lots of reasons. Alan is a really good man and does such a great job in all he does and I didn't want to spoil that, but for me, at that time, I felt that the man I was married to and living and working with, wasn't the same man that everyone else knew and appreciated. I just didn't like him. I wasn't 'in love' with him, wasn't sure I even loved him anymore and I didn't want to spend the rest of my life with him. But I didn't know how to begin to change things.

Things came to a head for me at a celebration service in September when a man shared his testimony and the pain he was going through because his wife of many years had walked out on him and their children – for no good reason, except that she had had enough. He pleaded with her and said what about their vows and she just said, "I wasn't a Christian then." This was so powerful for me, to see what damage I was thinking of inflicting on Alan and James, just because I had had enough, but what really spoke to me was that I too, was 'not a Christian when we married' – but God was still God and nothing can ever change that!

I spent the rest of that night in torment but awoke with peace in my heart. God brought us together before we knew Him, has kept us together and will keep us together until our times on this earth are done. I love Alan more now than ever. I don't need for him to use my name (but it's getting easier for him…) and I am proud of all that he does and has achieved.

Call out to God. He hears your cry and will bring you through everything that seems impossible to your eyes.

Coming up to Tom's fifth anniversary is strange. It's a milestone! We will never forget him. I am so proud of him, not for what he did but for what he has done since – he has touched thousands of lives through the telling of our story and given countless opportunities to show the love of God to so many people. I can never be cross or angry with him for taking his own life, because I understand a lot of how he felt, how he couldn't share it with anyone. I see that he poured it out in his poems but at the time I couldn't see what they meant to say. Yes, I would give anything to have him back but I believe his life would have been unhappy and if he hadn't taken his life at sixteen, he would have taken it at some later stage. In no way do I advocate suicide but I understand why people do it – even God loving Christians!!

January 2009

We have just come through the worst Christmas since Tom died.

Through November, as we settled back into work, I felt the pressure mounting of all that has to be done for Christmas and the extra work load that I have to do and just the commercialism of it all – Jesus doesn't get a look in anywhere!

The shop's third birthday was interesting – our first blazing row in twenty six years and plates thrown down the stairs by Alan (and cleared up by me as he'd stormed off – unheard of…). Matters not now, but it was all part of the tensions we were both feeling. Actually we were working really hard; the shop was busy; I was under the Christmas pressure that I mentioned and I was suffering from a panic attack. I had chest pains and trouble breathing. My legs were trembling and I didn't understand what was going on, only that I had people to feed and washing up to do.

I desperately wanted Alan to take the decision to 'close the shop' from me but he kept coming and asking what did I want to do – meanwhile more customers were coming in which meant more work…I thought I could soldier on and get through. I had felt similar on occasions before but not on this scale. I could not make the decision to close as I felt a failure and that I was letting us down. Anyway, Alan got really cross, closed the shop – and I am ashamed to admit – we rowed whilst there were still customers eating their lunches, which is when he threw the plates down the stairs…

I read an article, a year later, which described panic attacks exactly as I had experienced them and which said, it is just the body's response to extreme stress, saying it just cannot do anymore at that particular time and it needs to rest. I showed the article to Alan and reminded him of the year before. It helped us both to understand and we can actually laugh about that day now! I have since, on one or two occasions, felt a panic attack coming on and I am confident enough now to tell Alan how I feel. His caring response gives me strength and we work through it together – why could I not have shared more before?! We have both grown so much and trust each other so much more.

Through December I had the usual panic attacks, (not the same as I described above but where I am convinced something terrible is about to happen and I am powerless to stop it) only fleeting but there – going to see James in his room and 'seeing' him dead at his computer before I got to the top of the stairs. Someone left the loo light on at the shop and I expected to find a dead person in there, only two examples but real in my head and horrible at the time.

My mother passed out at a play at church and she was in exactly the same position as Tom was when I found him – head down, eyes open and nobody home. I still struggle with that one. I expect the worst when James is out and only relax when he comes home. I know that's a natural parent thing but its worse now; it will pass. Even this week, Alan had a tooth out in the morning and we were driving to Banbury in the afternoon and I'm expecting him to die because of the tooth. We laughed about it, thank God we can, but it's still real nonetheless.

Christmas Day, Alan had flu (real flu!!) and spent most of it in bed. James and I went to church. James was operating the data projector so he went early, and I felt so miserable I wasn't going to go. I only decided to go at the last minute and because of something I had shared in a testimony the week before.

For our Carols by Candlelight service Philip always has a testimony time, which is great, and usually relates to the last Alpha course, thereby plugging the next one. Phil had arranged someone to share their Alpha testimony but they were very poorly with flu and he wasn't sure if they would make it, so he asked us as plan B.

We put something together in the time we had – Sunday afternoon - and shared it at the service. I didn't think it flowed or was very good but then I never do! Anyway the gist was, *"Immanuel, God with us."* Alan shared about how we weren't Christians before Alpha 1999 and what the course meant to us and how we came to understand what Jesus did for us etc. I shared about Tom and how we now hate Christmas – because of what follows in January - and that it is only because of Phil saying on our first Christmas, after Tom died, that it is not about us but all about Jesus, that we get through and that is true of any difficult situation – *Turn your eyes upon Jesus, look full in His wonderful face, and the things of earth will grow strangely dim, in the light of His glory and grace."*

So that was the reason I made myself go to church on Christmas Day and I cried through most of the service but Jesus knew I was there and that I was there for Him. I left straight after, and James and I put flowers on Tom's grave and then I came home. I didn't feel miserable because Alan was ill but for myself – a deep misery that I couldn't explain.

Each Christmas Eve since, I've asked God to give me Tom back – even for a second – to turn the clock back and make everything right. Each Christmas morning I wake up and He hasn't done it and it hurts. I know He cannot do it. I know I am asking the impossible but it's like I tell Him on Christmas Eve what I'd like for Christmas and He doesn't give it to me and it aches deep in my soul. I know I will see Tom again one day and I know there will be no more pain or tears but just for that one moment – to be able to hold him, hug him, kiss him, just look at him – I would give anything!

Anyway, we had an okay time after that. Lunch was alright and our presents were lovely There was a moment when Alan had gone back to bed and James and I sat on the floor surrounded with wrapping paper and presents. That felt good – really good! We both felt it and enjoyed it but its taken four years. If you are reading this and relating to it, be kind to yourself, give yourself time. It will get better.

Friday 30<u>th</u> January 2009

The Fifth Anniversary of Tom's Suicide – horrid day!

It was a milestone to overcome and we knew we would, but it was still a difficult time. The whole week was, especially with it being a Friday. We found ourselves re-living the events of the same week, especially Thursday evening and Friday – remembering things we'd said and done with no clue as to what Tom was thinking. I am convinced he knew when he went to bed on Thursday night that he was going to take his life after school on Friday. Why didn't he do it on Thursday? I don't know, maybe to give us one last chance, maybe to say goodbye to his friends, maybe to take one last look at his world, who knows except him.

Anyway we decided we would work until 3:00pm and go over to Chipping Campden, put flowers on the grave for 5:30pm and have a cup of tea with Phil and then go out for dinner somewhere.

Getting up was strange as I remembered how he was on the morning five years ago. Alan and I both felt pangs as we saw the school bus go but once we were at the shop it was easier. In a way it was a release because we had both been at work and Tom had been at school and we hadn't given him a second thought as you don't when you think they're safe.

We were glad to close and finish up, as memories were building and we felt uneasy as the clock moved closer to 5:30pm. It was an unconscious thing but the feelings of knowing something terrible was going to happen and being powerless to stop it were almost overwhelming, more than ever they'd been before.

James met us at the shop and we drove to Chipping Campden, each thinking our own thoughts and saying little but deciding where we would go for dinner – an Indian restaurant we hadn't been to for a couple of years – James' idea. The flowers were beautiful and we placed them on the grave and thought about Tom with peace and sadness and then went to see Phil. By 6:00pm we were more relaxed as in a way the bad thing had happened, and here we were five years later – survivors thanks to the love of God and His people!

I read a book about coping with suicide. It recommended a party when you reached the five year anniversary – a 'surviving suicide' party. I thought about it but couldn't get my head around it so we didn't plan one but God (and probably Tom) had other ideas!!

Before we went for dinner we had a phone call from friends, inviting us for a meal in a couple of week's time. Alan mentioned where we were going and why, and thought no more of it, and the conversation ended and off we went.

We had just ordered our meal and were tucking into popadoms when who should enter the restaurant but the people whom Alan had been talking to. They felt we shouldn't be on our own, so came to join us for a drink. Their youngest son was with them and he did a very Tom thing and asked for some peppers from the waiter and ate one as if it was an apple, much to our amusement and his parents concern. Anyway, they couldn't stay long but it was just a lovely time and they left to pay for their drinks and our bill but we didn't know that then. We left that evening feeling very loved and very blessed by our heavenly Father and knew His arms were still around us. (Vanessa said she and John have never done anything like that before but felt it was very God and very right and we so love them for being obedient).

Just before Christmas we watched a DVD by Louis Giglio entitled *How Great Is Our God* – it is part of a series, another of which is *Indescribable*. They are awesome; you must see them, you cannot help but be inspired by the greatness of God. Anyway, the DVD ends with something which felt like it was written for us when I watched it and I feel it appropriate to end this book with it so I give all the credit to Louis and to God and hope I do it justice – some of the words I have taken straight off the film. It is based on Isaiah 40 which has meant so much to Alan and I the last five years – you will see why…

Louis defines waiting on God as being in the midst of the toughest place in your life, thinking you cannot take one more step, one more breath, but still trusting in God.

God doesn't always change the circumstances. He did not change them for Jesus but the cross is proof that God always has a purpose in the circumstances and that His purpose and plan will prevail and will triumph through any circumstances in this world.

Remember Isaiah 40v28, *Do you not know? Have you not heard? The Lord is the everlasting God, the Creator of the ends of the earth. He will not grow tired or weary and His understanding no-one can fathom. He gives strength to the weary and increases the power of the weak.*

Even youths grow tired and weary and young men stumble and fall but those who hope in the Lord will renew their strength. They will soar on wings like eagles; they will run and not grow weary; they will walk and not be faint.

The Hebrew meaning of 'hope/wait' means 'those who stand in the midst of the craziness and pain and chaos and right in the valley of the shadow of death', and they don't gloss over it – they are dealing with the hardest stuff in their lives. (This is exactly how I felt so many times through the last few years). But right in the middle of it, they say, "I don't see or understand what God is doing. I don't see what the plan is but I am not going to give up on God and I am going to trust that He has a plan and a purpose for my life. I believe I am going to see the goodness of God in the land of the living and I am not going to stop believing that no matter what." That is what 'to hope' means.

The promise is not to wake up to rosy circumstances – He can do that and He does do that but the promise is greater than that. He says, *Those who wait on the Lord I will renew their strength. When you think you can't take one more breath, I will lift you up and give you enough to keep going on. You will feel like you have been swept up on the wings of eagles. You will run and not grow weary and you will walk through it all and not faint. I will hold you. Even when you let go of Me I will not let go of you." That is the promise of the everlasting God.*

Remember back at the beginning of it all – Monday evening – and the picture I had of being carried over the canyon/valley on the wings of eagles? Our wonderful Father God keeps His promises, every single one. Sometimes it is only when we look back that we can see. He gave me a new picture in June '08. The talk was from Rob White, based on 1 Samuel 14, where Jonathon and his armour-bearer climbed up the side of a mountain and defeated their enemy. Rob asked the question, "What is our next mountain-top view? – We've reached the top of one. Are we complacent or are we looking for the next?" My picture was clear. I was at the top reaching down to those in the same valley that we had been through and helping them up. I was looking back – but with a purpose and with faith.

I pray that through this journal and account of everything we have been through since Tom died, that you will see how wonderful and amazing our God is, how He lifts and carries us and sets us free to soar on wings like eagles, to glorify Him.

I used to think God was arrogant, to want us to spend eternity praising and worshipping Him, but through all we've experienced I cannot wait – to stand before Him in Heaven and know I've done all I could to sing of His great love for us here on earth. What else is our life for?

And yet, I'm not ready. There's too much else to do. We haven't yet done all that we can but time is running out – Where do you stand? Do you know Him? (Do you want to know Him as a result of reading this book? Then do an Alpha course...) Do you love Him? Do you serve Him daily with your whole body, mind and strength? (I don't – but I want to...) Do you long to see His kingdom come on this earth? Do you long to see others come to know Him as you do? Where do you stand...?

My prayer for this journal is for everyone who reads it to be touched by the glory of God, through the text or through the poems. I pray that if only one person is helped by something that I have shared then this whole book will have been worth every ounce of pain that is held within it.

God Bless. See you later.

I Wonder...

I wonder if you consider...
The Creator of all things, above and below,
The wonder of nature, the uniqueness of snow,
The sun and the moon and the stars in between,
All things that are hidden and those that are seen.

I wonder do you believe...
In His Power, His Glory, His infinite Might,
His unceasing delivering by day and by night,
All things brought to order from His heavenly Throne,
So lovingly cared for and known as His own.

I wonder will you receive...
His Mercy, His Compassion, His amazing Grace,
Will you trust Him forever; seek naught but His Face,
Give your life up to follow His Heart and His Ways –
A life of excitement, fellowship and praise.

I wonder will you rest...
In His Love, in His Wisdom, His Word and His Strength,
When times are dark and faith is put to the test,
When troubles abound in your too busy life,
Will you live in His Peace – His Grace will suffice.

I wonder will you love...
As much as He loves you – unconditional,
Unfailing, faithful and true,
You'll never deserve it, nor earn it, nor pay any fee,
You can simply receive it, it's given for free.

I wonder will you see...
With your eyes bright and clear,
Will you open your ears, be able to hear
The wonderful message He has for you,
He made you; He loves you – what more can He do?

He sent you His Son to die on a cross,
Alone and in agony so you'd not be lost.
Your sins on His shoulders too heavy to bear –
How else could He show you His love and His care?
Your Father in Heaven, calls you by name,
Knows all of your struggles, your heartache and pain,
Shares all of your laughter, your joys and your cares,
Watches over your nights while you sleep unaware.
How awesome His love is, how tender and sweet,
How immense and how strong and wonderfully complete.

I wonder do you get it...
Has it sunk into your head?
Simply follow your heart, by His Spirit be led.
Believe in your Father, in Jesus His Son,
For your Salvation, God's Victory was won.

Jackie. 13. April 2008

I wrote this one Sunday Morning when I didn't want to be at Church, didn't want to face anyone, least of all God. I didn't feel I could mean what I sang to Him. As I sat on my own before the service, I found myself asking why I was there if I really didn't want to be. As I thought I realised I was 'thinking in rhyme' so again, as happened so often before, the poem wrote itself. I stayed for the service and wrote the poem when we got home, having 'lived it'. I gave a copy to Phil and he used it in a sermon on worship and it was a blessing to many of the congregation.

Sacrifice of Praise

Why am I here, why did I come?
I need to stay but I want to run,
I can't face my friends – I just want to hide,
I've nothing to give and I'm empty inside.
I feel so helpless, so weak and so small,
The words of the songs cause tears to fall –
Silently, discreetly so no-one can see
The pain I am feeling – why's it just me?
Everyone else is joyful in praise,
My arms feel like lead – too heavy to raise.
My eyes are downcast, fixed on myself,
I'm drowning in sorrow above all else.
But God is still God, He knows my need
And Jesus still died – gave His life up for me,
And little by little as I look to His face
I'm lifted right up and bathed in His grace.
I can lift up my voice, my heart and my hands,
Surrender forever my life to His plans.
I'm lost in His beauty, His peace and His love,
I'm lifted in wonder to glimpse heaven above,
To worship my Father, my Saviour, my Lord,
To soar in His presence, as free as a bird.
For this I was born, for this I was made –
I'm so glad I came, I'm so glad I stayed.

Jackie. 15. March 2009

I wrote this poem on Mother's Day, after I was encouraged by someone that it was time to move on. I had been sharing how difficult days like that still are — and it was difficult to share with that person — how painful I still find them. James is wonderful and makes me feel so special but there will always be someone missing and I feel guilty for James that he has to make up for being the only son (he doesn't have to at all). I was very hurt by the comment about moving on and was about to open my mouth and give a very stinging reply but grace prevailed and I just let it go. But I still had hurt feelings to deal with — hence the poem…

The Loss of a Child

When you lose your child, life doesn't make sense,
You are cut to the core, your grief is immense.
It's a different hurt for a sister or brother,
How much more for a father or mother?

We don't need to hear that 'time will heal',
You don't know our pain or how we feel,
Please don't tell us 'it's time to move on',
It's not your child who died, or your loved one who's gone.

When we wrap ourselves in a burden of guilt —
Real or imagined it's what we've each felt;
Should have seen it, stopped it, been there, and done more…
Please hear us, don't judge us, please don't ignore

The cries of our hearts for lives that are gone,
We need your compassion to help us stay strong.
So love us, walk with us — be it one year or five,
Encourage us to talk — keep the memories alive,

Surround us with prayer, with love and with grace,
Point us to Jesus — help us look to His face,
He'll restore and renew us; He'll show us His care
Because safe in His kingdom, our children are there.

Jackie. 23. March 2009

I wrote this after an amazing evening service, when the worship time was so awesome and timeless and I felt we could all have been singing with the angels in heaven – it really was as I've described!

A Glimpse of Heaven

Standing all together
Our voices raised as one,
Singing praises to our Saviour,
Jesus, Holy One.

Musicians lift and carry us
To a higher and beautiful place,
Before the Throne of God above,
Beholding Jesus' face.

Holy Spirit fills and leads us.
Prayers rise and fall,
Souls aflame – no holding back,
Giving glory to our Lord.

We're captured by His beauty,
Enfolded in His love –
Oh! To stay in this place forever,
Reaching out to heaven above.

Is this what we'll feel when we get there?
Is this what it's all about?
Perfect peace, endless joy,
No pain, no guilt, no doubt!

Joining with the angels,
Myriad voices singing praise,
Giving joyful Hallelujah's
Under Jesus' adoring gaze.

Thank You for this blessing,
This glimpse of heaven for free.
Use us for Your glory Lord,
'Till we're Yours for eternity.

Jackie. 18. May 2009

Why Tom?

This part of our story is probably the most difficult to write: why Tom took his life, but we each feel it is important to include as much information as possible and who better to write that information but Tom himself. You will remember, at the beginning of my story, we found what he called his 'suicide file' which we read and it helped us to understand a little about why he did what he did. He poured himself out on paper in a way that he could not do to us or anyone – I understand that so well, as I too was unable to share my deepest thoughts and fears with anyone. If I had, maybe things wouldn't have seemed so bad – a problem shared and all that – but the truth is that although I was surrounded by loving and caring people I just could not open myself up to be vulnerable and to the possibility of ridicule as I saw it. So I would make excuses in my head as to why I couldn't talk to my friends or even Phil who had walked every step with us. I guess he felt the same, so Tom and I kept everything deep inside invisible to everyone except God.

The obvious thing to say here is that there is ALWAYS someone that you can talk to. It may initially be really hard to approach someone and to say what you are going through, to be really vulnerable and honest but it will be worth it because they will take you seriously. They will listen and they will be able to help and if they are true Christian people they will pray with you and for you and lift your situation to the One who cares above all.

So, back to Tom! We feel it right to include as much of what he wrote in the last few months. There will inevitably be some omissions, things relevant to his close friends that may cause pain if they were to be included, and a lot of swear words which I shall probably just disguise!

Tom states somewhere that he felt he never fitted in – and in a way he didn't. He was mature way beyond his years, even from a young age. He could carry on a good intelligent conversation with adults and yet not quite fit with his peers. He was often bullied for no reason. Once, in a country park somewhere, he and James were just minding their own business watching some animals and a child, much younger than they, came out of nowhere and thumped Tom and ran off. I wouldn't have believed it if I hadn't seen it! At junior school he was verbally bullied and teased by his classmates (which the school did not take seriously and he was told to 'put up or shut up' by a senior teacher). One afternoon, as we walked home, I asked him how his day had been and he mentioned suicide for the first time. I don't remember his exact words or my reply but I think we talked about how he felt about the bullying and I tried to encourage him to be strong and ignore it. This would have been probably in his final year before going to secondary school.

When the class went to the secondary school for a two day visit, there was a scuffle between Tom and his antagonists and he thumped one of them. This resulted in a stern talk by the lady who was to be their Head of Year, who encouraged Tom to work very hard at it not mattering, whilst they (the teachers and the school) would work very hard at it not happening. I am grateful to that lady teacher for taking Tom and the situation seriously and jumping on it straight away.

Once he had started at senior school, Tom didn't mention being called names again and we thought that was the end of it. However, one afternoon, on the bus, on the way home, the boy in the seat behind put his tie around Tom's neck and strangled him, so much that he became unconscious for a few minutes. Apparently this was an 'initiation ceremony' and the boy who did it to Tom had had it done to him. Tom was able to tell us about this episode and we dealt with it straight away. I was able to speak to the boy's mother, who was mortified that her son had done this and punished him accordingly. We spoke with the school who were able to prevent it happening again – they put 'monitors' in charge on the buses (6th formers) and kids were told in no uncertain terms what would happen if this behaviour continued. I have no idea if this is what put the idea of hanging into Tom's head but it's not something he would ever have forgotten.

He never mentioned being bullied again so we assumed that it was all over with. As he went through the years at school he did really well academically – he was predicted A*s for his GCSE's. He never seemed to struggle with homework (in fact he hardly seemed to do any at home. He managed to get it done at school). He was completely opposite to James, who had to work hard to achieve the results that he did but Tom just seemed to breeze through and hardly work at all! He built up some really strong friendships – especially in his last years there. He had an amazing group of friends who were supportive of each other – and to us after his death.

As any young man would, Tom struggled with surging hormones and how to deal with the feelings that came with that part of growing up. He couldn't talk to us – well you don't talk to your parents about that, do you? I tried to talk with him about girls and stuff, especially once he had met his girlfriend (who was and still is a wonderful girl, whom I love and I am so grateful to her that Tom experienced a loving relationship, even though it was only for a short time).

You will see from his letters how much that side of things took over his thinking with a passion that he could not begin to deal with. It has been a difficult decision to include a lot of what he wrote – names have been changed or left out – because we don't want the people he writes about (his close friends) to ever be hurt in any way – they were not at all responsible and our fear is that they may read this someday and think that they were – just by being the friends that they were.

However, we feel we have to include everything to give a complete picture of Tom's mind and situations that led him to take his life and that means the hard stuff about myself. He says things that hurt and if I am honest, there were signs – I just didn't know what to do with them. So I tried my best to talk with him and get him to open up and I really thought he would come through this difficult time in his life but he couldn't and wouldn't talk to me. I don't think we liked each other very much at that point and we certainly didn't understand each other. I did tell him that once not long before he died, but I did tell him that I loved him.

We want to start by giving a picture of the carefree boy that he was when he was thirteen and building up to the thoughts that caused him to end his life. As I have said he was an inspired and gifted writer, of poetry but also stories, which I cannot include because of their length but which gripped you from the opening sentence to the closing chapter. I used to love to watch him when he was writing. He would type so fast and furiously, his fingers just flying over the keypad and his eyes on the screen. It was no good trying to get any sense out of him until he had finished but it was so worth waiting for, whether short or long, funny or profound.

When the writing got darker, we understood less, couldn't get where he was coming from as outwardly there was no change and he couldn't begin to tell us what was going on inside his head. When we did ask, he would just shrug and say everything was fine – so we had to believe him and trust that he was okay.

To re-visit these letters has been painful and emotional – but also healing. It has been an enormous mental effort to begin. I know the devil will do anything to stop me but I firmly believe that there will be something that will help parents of children of all ages, to see inside the mind of a suicide victim, a 'normal' sixteen year old. My fear is that some people may read it in a 'voyeuristic' way but that is not our intention at all. As with the whole book, our prayer is that someone, somewhere will be touched, healed, saved (in more ways than one) inspired and encouraged by the telling of our story, not for our benefit but entirely for the glory of God with whom Tom is safely waiting for us. If just one family is able to talk and communicate with each other better as a result of their parents reading this, then it is more than worth it.

Some things are dated, others are not, but I have tried to put them into a logical order as when they were written but they may have been shuffled around a little and not be entirely in the right order.

I Have a Dream

I have a dream where there's never a fight
So everyone's happy and the attitude's right
There's never disease and everyone's well
So it's only Heaven and never Hell.

There aren't any wars so no one dies
And no-one cheats and no-one lies
Everyone smiles and they never cry
And they never ponder over who, where or why.

They do what they have to and would never be late
And don't know the meaning of the horrid word "hate"
Why aren't we like that, never fight, never lie?
If we could all change less people would die.

For this isn't a dream, it's a forgotten reality
There's so much violence it's nearing totality
So how long will it be before war reaches the top?
I have a Dream that all hatred will stop.

©Tom Slough
23rd September 1999

A Rainy Day

Mummy, when will it stop raining?
I want to go out and play,
You said it would stop in half an hour,
And that was last Saturday!

I'll wear my wellington boots, Mummy,
I'll wear my heavy raincoat,
I'll even wear a big rubber ring,
So if I fall in a puddle I'll float!

Oh, why can't I go out and play Mummy?
If I can't I'll have to get mad,
And you know what happens when I'm bored and annoyed,
I start to be very bad!

I'll jump on the chairs and draw on the walls,
I'll shout and I'll scream and I'll curse,
And if I still can't go out and play,
My tantrum will have to get worse!

What's that you say? It's stopped raining?
Whoopee, I can go out and play,
Until, that is, it rains again,
But that's for another day!

© Tom Slough

6th May 2000

A Soldier's Story

A man died on a cross last week,
He called himself a King,
The King of the Jews, the Lord's own Son,
And about Him now I sing,

Of course, no one believed Him,
Though He performed impossible things,
He turned water to wine and raised the dead,
And about Him now I sing,

He had a dozen followers,
His Disciples, His inner ring,
Many other people loved Him,
And about Him now I sing,

The priests all wanted Him murdered,
They plotted against the King,
They bribed a Disciple with silver coins,
And about Him now I sing,

This Disciple betrayed his friend with a kiss,
He did it to show he was king,
The man was taken off by my soldiers,
And about Him now I sing,

They flogged Him and they beat Him,
Then they crucified the King,
He cried, "It is finished!" and drew His last breath,
And about Him now I sing,

His name was Jesus, that man they killed,
He was the Son of God, and a King,
For He has risen from the grave,
And about Him I will sing.

As the Clock Strikes Twelve

As the clock strikes twelve, we enter new time,
New problems, new answers, new music and rhyme.
As the clock strikes twelve, 2000 years passed,
Since God's Son was born, His first and His last.

As the clock strikes twelve, the race has begun,
For the millennium daughter or millennium son.
As the clock strikes twelve, we learn from the past,
With thoughts for the future, as time moves on fast.

As the clock strikes twelve, we remember some more,
About people who died for their country in war.
As the clock strikes twelve, we can feel the power,
The power of love in this sacred hour.

As the clock strikes twelve, think of the poor,
In countries where poverty should be no more.
As the clock strikes twelve, just hear my plea,
Help the needy, if not for them, then for me.

©Tom Slough
31st December 2000

Jackie Slough

Ask the World a Question

Ask the world a question,
Try asking the world why,
Just ask the world this question,
When the world is passing by,

Why food abounds in plenty,
Yet thousands go without,
Why all the world is crying,
But we never hear its shout,

Why the world is plunged in darkness,
Full of crime and full of sin,
Why the poor are knocking at your door,
But you never let them in,

Why so few have so much in life,
Yet millions have none,
Why some can rest by pools; and yet,
Men blister in the sun,

And yet, through this there's a glimmer of light,
That wipes out famine and sword,
That hope is the love of Jesus Christ,
Our Saviour and risen Lord.

My Invisible Friend

I have an invisible friend, who's a bear,
And he eats invisible honey,
Which he buys at the invisible Kwik-e-mart,
Where he spends his invisible money.

He eats it off an invisible plate,
That's as wide as it is long,
And when he's finished his invisible meal,
He sings this invisible song:

Oh, rinkle tinkle tangy doo,
I'm invisible and you are too,
Oh rinkle tinkle tangy dee,
I can't see you and you can't see me!

And when he's finished his invisible song,
He has an invisible nap,
And when he wakes up he goes on a walk,
Wearing his invisible cap.

When he's in the Park he's very bad,
But no one sees a thing,
And when he's done enough mischief,
He has an invisible sing:

Oh rinkle tinkle tangy doo,
I'm invisible and so are you,
Oh rinkle tinkle tangy dee,
I can't see you and you can't see me!

© Tom Slough

It's Not Fair!

Mummy, I can't act grown up!
I'm not an adult yet,
I can't have a drink down at the pub,
I can't drive or place a bet!

You want me to set an example,
Well, I think that you've been had,
You see, I'm already setting one,
It's just the one that I'm setting is bad!

It's not fair for me to have to be good,
You act like a baby as well,
If you don't get what you want done,
You throw a tantrum and yell!

I don't like being the eldest!
Life's rubbish and you know its true,
I'm too young to do anything fun,
And I can't argue back at you!

Why should I be the perfect child?
Brave and handsome and bold,
You can't expect me to act grown up,
I'm only six years old!

© Tom Slough

June 2000

God

God is a bit like a person who has volunteered for a magic trick and is made to disappear – no one can see him, but most know he is there and has not vanished at all, but is merely invisible. Some people, however, will see nothing and therefore believe there is nothing there.

The devil is like the magician. He makes God disappear before people, and convinces them that there is nothing there. He will trick anyone he can, and that is when he rewards himself, like the magician getting paid.

Which would you rather be? The people who know that God is there or the ones who believe He has gone or never existed?

©Tom Slough 2001

In the Imagination of a Child

Pray tell, kind sir, please answer me

Whom shall I be today?

Perhaps a clever scholar,

Or a playwright with his play?

Maybe I'll be a warrior, honest, brave and bold,

Or perhaps the gentle woodsman who keeps the lore of old.

A paladin, a champion, who's sword defends what's right?

Renowned for feats of bravery, courageous, strong and bright?

Perhaps I'm from the future, from the time when the world ends.

With just three hours to save the world – with just some chosen friends!

No, I've decided who it is that today I want to be.

It's the person I want to be the most and that person

Is Me.

My New Pet

I saw a little monster,
It was hiding down a drain,
I think it had got washed down there,
The last time it had rained.

Its fuzzy coat was like a dog,
Its eyes were very small,
Its little mouth was like a rat,
Its claws were on the wall.

I pulled up the drain and fished it out,
It shook its purple hair,
It's now living in with the dog,
And it will be staying there!

My mum really hates it,
My brother thinks its cool,
My dad says it will be hard to keep,
But I think he's a fool.

It might look evil with its red eyes,
But it wouldn't hurt a fly,
It's really the cutest little dear,
It makes me want to cry!

©Tom Slough
21st June 2000

Seeking

A man was wandering around in the basement of his house. He didn't know why he was down there, but as he was there he decided to clean it out.

He tidied around, not really doing anything still – just moving piles of newspaper across the room and back again to see what was under them.

About two hours later the basement looked virtually exactly the same. Then, he made up his mind to do what he'd gone down there to do and not come out until the basement was tidy. So he put some music on and buckled down to some hard work.

Later, he found a trunk that looked really old. There was a padlock on it, and the man wondered if a key he'd had for years but didn't fit any locks would go in that one.

He dug the key out of a drawer and took it to the trunk. Fitting it in, he started to turn it. The lock was stiff and hard to turn at first, but it got easier.

The lock clicked and the man opened the trunk. He gasped. It contained his oldest toys that he thought had been lost forever. That was the best thing in his week.

That man is like someone searching for God – he doesn't know it, but he is desperate to find it. If he went to Church, he wouldn't be any nearer. He would still be searching.

It is only when he really listens to the service that he finds the key – PRAYER.

When that has unlocked God for that person, it will be the best thing in his life.

© Tom Slough

The Walk

A man, having just moved house, decided to go on a walk. Being quite a keen walker, he had soon travelled all the footpaths in the area except one. After two weeks he felt so curious about that footpath he set off down it almost immediately after breakfast, taking nothing with him except the clothes he wore.

It was a hard path to travel, with lots of twists and turns. In some places it was so overgrown that the man could hardly get through. He could have just turned round and gone back, but he didn't because he wanted to find out where the path led.

Sometimes the other paths he'd travelled along crossed this one: He could have travelled back along one of those but again he didn't.

It was late in the day and the man was tired. He had walked all day and had missed lunch, but still hadn't reached the end. Then, it started to rain heavily. Soon a mighty storm was happening, and the man was soaked to the skin.

A light appeared somewhere: a door had been opened and the man could just make out the shape of a farmer hurrying down towards him. This farmer took him inside his house and gave him food, drink and a change of clothes. He let the man stay there overnight, and for as long as it took for the storm and the rain to stop.

Next morning the sun was shining brightly. The man left the farmhouse and its kind owner after asking for directions and within an hour was home.

We are that man. The path we walk is the path to God. Sometimes it is the hardest to travel and we want to turn back, and sometimes we are sorely tempted to take the easy way out.

But if we stick to the path then God will help and shelter us through stormy times, and we will receive our reward at the end.

© Tom Slough 2000

The Battle of Troy

The battle began as the Greek soldier roared,
And the archers pulled back their bowstrings and poured
Their deadly shafts on the enemy head,
Till many were injured and many were dead.

Then the cavalry charged towards their foe,
But many were felled by the enemy bow,
Yet still they charged on, regardless of danger,
Friend by friend and stranger with stranger.

And then the Greeks met the opposing force,
And man killed man and man killed horse,
Some cowardly soldiers turned and ran,
As the battle for life and death began.

As the battle raged on for a lady fair,
The screams of the dying filled the air.
Then the next charge began, larger than the last,
The swordsmen ran on, surefooted and fast.

They sprinted on down the side of the hill,
Each sword raised high to maim and kill.
And as a fearsome battle cry escaped each mouth,
The enemy turned and retreated back south.

Back to their castle, a symbol of power,
Where the lady watched from high in a tower,
That lady who'd run off with a teenage boy,
That lovely lady, who was Helen of Troy.

As the battle went on by the river of Troy,
Every man sought to kill and destroy,
As the battle went on for the Greeks pride,
Helen herself watched from inside,

Until many months later when hundreds were dead,
The Greeks stopped fighting and sailed instead,
Off down the river, to the sea on it's course,
Leaving some troops behind, in a wooden horse.

© Tom Slough 2000

The Night Before Christmas (or 'There's no such thing as Santa but my Children think there is')

'Twas the night before Christmas, and all through the house,
Not a creature was stirring, not even a mouse,
My children were sleeping, one girl and two boys,
Hoping Saint Nicholas would soon bring them toys,

The clock in the hallway struck one in the morn,
As I got out of bed and stifled a yawn,
The floor creaked beneath me as I crept to the shelves,
And reached for the toys made by Santa's "elves".

I counted the toys, to make sure of them all
Then carried them out on my back to the hall,
I ate both the mince pies – boy, were they good!
And got tipsy on sherry, as Santa Claus would.

I crept to my son's room, and up to his chair,
And I left him some toys in the stocking hung there,
My youngest son next; his room wasn't far,
I left in his stocking a big model car.

My daughter had wanted a real life horse,
But it wouldn't have fit in my sack, of course,
So I left her a Rudolph with a big shiny nose,
And into the hallway I sneaked on my toes.

Then down the stairs I swiftly did flee,
And scattered the last gifts around the tree,
And as I went back to bed, late on Christmas night,
I whispered to my children, "Saint Nick says good night."

The Man On The Cross

Now I've seen some pretty strange things in my career in the Roman army, but nothing prepared me for what happened five days ago. As I remember, it was the story of the man on the cross…

'It was coming up to the time of the Passover – the major Jewish festival of the year. I never went in for all that nonsense, but I was stationed in Jerusalem in case any riots or street fights occurred. The Jews all migrate to Jerusalem for the festival, but this year a mad rumour was going round that spread like wildfire. Everywhere you went people were whispering, "He's coming, Jesus of Nazareth is coming to Jerusalem!"

I'd heard about this man – Jesus of Nazareth, the Son of God – a performer of miracles, and the priests had it in for him. I wasn't particularly interested in him, but it would make things interesting to see him confront the Pharisees.

Well, Jesus came. Not riding on a fine white stallion like everyone expected, but on a donkey. A Donkey! Here was the supposed king of the Jews, and all he could ride on was a donkey? I laughed, but the crowd went wild, shouting, "Hosanna" and covering the ground before him with palm leaves and their cloaks.

Needless to say, there wasn't a riot or a revolt, and the next few days went by without any mention of Jesus. That was until last Thursday, when my commanding officer orders my platoon to accompany the Pharisees to the Garden of Gethsemane, where we were to arrest Jesus of Nazareth. Arrest him! So the conflict I had predicted was about to happen.

We marched along in the dead of night with the Pharisees and a man named Judas Iscariot. I learned that this man was one of Jesus' disciples who had betrayed him for thirty silver pieces.

Soon, we reached the garden, and there found Jesus praying, with four of his other disciples asleep.

*J*udas went up to Jesus and kissed him, and that was the signal. My men surged forwards to arrest Jesus with me in front, and the disciples woke up.

One was less sleepy than the others were – Peter, I think he was called – and he leaped forward, sword in hand. Before I knew what was happening, the air was ringing with screams of pain as Peter sliced through the ear of one of the soldiers.

"Peter." It was Jesus. "Do you not think my Father could have sent ten legions of angels to defend me? This is how it is meant to be: put away your sword." Then, taking the soldiers' head in his hands, he looked in his eyes. Looking across, I saw such love, sympathy and understanding I had never before seen in someone – this Jesus radiated humility. Covering the soldier's ear with his hand, he rubbed it gently. It was healed.

I felt a new respect for this man, but it soon faded. I had to arrest him as that was the orders I had been given. I tied his wrists, and we marched him off between us.

I stood guard outside the courtroom while Jesus was tried before Pilate, and then escorted him off to Herod. Another long hour as sentry there, then back to Pilate. By this time the sun was up and a crowd was gathering in the courtyard. I marched Jesus up to the balcony where Pilate was surveying the crowd, and this time got to stay and watch.

"People," began Pilate, "I can not think what this man has done wrong – please tell me if you know?" Instantly the cry came back:
"He says he's God!"
"He's a blasphemer!"
I looked out into that crowd, and saw hate, spite and malice on some of the faces where before there had been love and adoration for this man.

The trial went on for at least an hour, and then Pilate said,
 "I've had enough of this! I wash my hands of the whole matter! Do with this man what you want!" Then he stormed from the balcony.

Once again, I took a direct part in Jesus' time in Jerusalem – I was one of the two chosen to flog him. Of course, I let the others have their fun first.

Firstly, they got a scarlet cloak and wrapped it round him, jeering and mockingly calling him king. Then, they forced a crown of thorns onto his head, so tightly it caused blood to trickle into his eyes. Then came the flogging.

We used special rods, and lashed him fifty times, so the keen whips had scoured off most of his back. Those eyes that had been filled with love and compassion were now clouded with pain and anguish. I was forced to look away, but the worst was to come. He was to be crucified on Calvary hill, just outside the city.

Jesus hobbled along, forced to carry the massive crosspiece on which he would later die. I was told to 'help' him along with blows from my spear butt if he fell, which he did quite often. Finally, too exhausted to move, he collapsed on the road. I called a man from the crowd to help him carry the cross, and so Jesus made it to the hill.

The other part of the cross was already there, and while the soldiers fixed the other piece to it, Jesus was able to gain his breath. When the cross was assembled, they came across to us and dragged Jesus to it. Laying him down flat, they held his wrist out … and handed me the nails.

Now most people scream and struggle as we put the nails in but he just turned and looked at me, his eyes clouded with pain. Tears welled up in my eyes, and all I could do was to whisper to him, "Sorry." He nodded. I raised the hammer and struck the nail home into his wrist and he didn't even scream. I almost wished he had.

They hauled up the cross, and hung him there for hour upon hour. There were women crying, and I recognised the four disciples who'd been there at the arrest, weeping bitterly. I almost cried myself.

The hours passed and the sky darkened. Jesus cried in pain, and yelled out to the darkened sky, "Father – It is Finished!" His head slumped down, dead. I couldn't help it, I fell to my knees and cried "Jesus – You are the Lord! You are the Son of God!" then, still on my knees, I wept bitterly.

They say he's risen. It happened on Sunday, when the tomb was found empty – there was talk of angels. The authorities say it was just grave robbers, though.

One thing's for certain – no matter how long I live, I'll always remember the Man on the Cross.

True life

Life is only good when you are having fun: appreciate the number of good times you have even in the bad ones.

If you think life is unfair, think again. You have got a home, money, good food,
Clean water and your good health.

Be grateful for what you have and think of others with less or none of it.

Poverty is bad. Accompanied with hunger, thirst and disease, it is terrible.

If you are rich, give to the poor. If you are poor, be thankful for what you get.

No matter how bad you think things are, remember that someone is usually worse off than you are.

Money can lead to greed: friendship and love are the only ways to true happiness.

Money is harmless: it's what you do with it that can be bad.

If you buy your food, think of the people who depend on the weather to survive from starvation.

Developing countries are poor. Undeveloped ones are even worse off.

Even the lushest city has poverty and sin within its boundaries.

Third world countries can be like ours: give them the chance to become what they can be.

A crisis at home is never as big if you think of the disasters in some countries

Modern methods have improved many lives yet ruined many others. A nice warm bed, a decent meal: mere fantasies for some people in the third world countries. Why not help them become reality?

With questioning comes the truth: children can be far better at finding it than adults are.

Adults accept things as they are – a child will question it and why it has to be like that.

The gift of an enquiring mind is far better than any present that can be given.

The future generation can often reveal more about the present one.

No Regrets

She is the most beautiful girl I know, and she really likes me.
There's one small problem; she doesn't want to go out with me.
I asked her out today, and she didn't answer.
No regrets.
She sort of panicked, and didn't answer me before the lesson.
I gave her some time to think about it.
She couldn't answer me in person – one of her friends told me.
I'd almost been able to guess the answer beforehand.
"She really likes you, but the problem is…" that was the best part.
"The problem is there's this other boy who likes her…" bastard.
"There's this other boy who likes her and she doesn't like him…"
"She doesn't want to go out with him"… another good part.
"But she feels it would be unfair for her to go out with you…"
"And plus, she doesn't really want a boyfriend at the moment."
Why the hell couldn't her friend have said just that?
She avoided me for the rest of the day.
She wasn't where she usually was at lunch.
She wasn't with whom she was usually with at lunch.
I'm just hoping she wasn't feeling embarrassed by me.
I've got the same lessons tomorrow.
The same order.
Science, and then History.
I sit next to her in Science.
Couldn't work up enough courage to ask her then.
Had to ask her before History.
Had to pray for the courage to ask her.
God gave it to me – I couldn't have done it otherwise
Prayed more today about it.
No regrets.
Except, perhaps about her answer.
Had to pray for self-control afterwards.
Didn't want to get angry.
Strange thing was, it didn't hurt at first.
Hurt like hell after an hour or two.

Had to pray for compassion.
Didn't want to end up embittered.
Didn't want to end up hating her.
At least, I don't want to lose her friendship.
No regrets.
I still like her as much as before.
She's still the most beautiful girl I know.
She's still the girl I want to go out with.
At least I don't hate her.
No regrets.
Can't help but think about what might have been.
What if I'd asked her out in a different way?
What if I'd asked her out later in the year?
But it probably wouldn't have made any difference.
I can't help but hope when the phone rings.
It's my overactive imagination, no doubt.
Keep hoping against hope that she looked up my number
Keep hoping she's phoned to say she takes it back.
That she does really like me.
That she does want to go out with me.
I got a text message in Tech today.
Hoped against hope it was her, or her friends.
Ignored the fact that she wouldn't have my number
It was a network message.
"Network message, please delete".
No regrets.
I know who the other boy is, I think.
One of my friends sits on the other side of her.
One lesson, she went on and on about this boy.
Tried to convince her to go out with him.
She got annoyed.
I thought it a slightly good sign.
No regrets.
Poured out my heart on to paper, in this poem.
Don't really know how to speak to my parents about it.
They wouldn't really understand about it, I don't think.
They'd just say I didn't need a girlfriend.

My mother would, anyway.
They probably can't remember what it was like.
To live as I live now.
No regrets.
Spoken to God about it countless times.
Poured out my heart to Him in prayer.
It really is quiet, walking the dogs.
Perfect for some heartfelt prayers.
No regrets.
I still like her.
I hope against hope for many things.
That the "She really likes you" came from her.
That it wasn't invented to try and make me feel better.
God will help me through.
No regrets.
I don't feel self-expressing enough to tell my parents this.
Ink is my medium.
A4 is my canvas.
Paintings show the artists feelings through brush-strokes.
Literature shows its author's feelings through letters.
I couldn't say all this out loud.
No regrets.
Music can help feelings too.
Walk the dogs, get home.
Feeling of pent-up frustration still lingers.
Go up to my room, and listen to some music that mirrors my feelings.
Queen and Meatloaf. Great for releasing emotion.
Bat out of Hell. As fast as my hopes vanished.
The Show Must Go On. It must indeed.
Full volume – with earphones so as not to disturb the parents.
Maybe not good for the hearing.
Can do a hell of a lot for the nerves, though.
No regrets.
I couldn't regret asking her out today.
No regrets.
None at all.
No regrets.

Tom Slough.

5th December 2002

Ashes

Ever wonder what it was you had
Before you were a chunk of world gone bad,
The life you led, the friends you knew
The love and warmth that made me love you.
But all that's gone, you don't know why
And you see the clouds turn to ashes in the sky.

Ashes to ashes, dust to dust
You need someone to turn to, someone to trust,
While all other people turn and flee,
Those ashes to ashes are banished by me.

You've run from shelter
You've run from truth
While all you need is a compassionate roof.
You had so much but threw it away
For a few precious moments of passionate play.
You're limping behind as we all fly south
And good food turns to ashes in your mouth.

Ashes to Ashes, dust to dust
You need someone to turn to, someone to trust,
While all other people turn and flee,
Those Ashes to Ashes are banished by me.

Ashes to ashes, you just hide your past
Those ashes to ashes will vanish at last
Ashes to ashes, hold tight to me
Those ashes to ashes will set us both free.

Ashes to ashes, dust to dust
You need someone to turn to, someone to trust,
While all other people turn and flee,
Those ashes to ashes are banished by me.

Last Release

Shooting at nothing
Staring at you
Wishing for someone
To make this come true
Looking for freedom
Searching for truth
Finally found you
At the fountain of youth.

Finally found our real lives
Hidden in the truth and lies
Looking for your sense of peace
I finally found our last release.

Crying my mind out
Hearing your cries
Looking for wisdom
From words of the wise
Needing more from it
I'm fading away
I need someone by me
When no-one else stays.

Finally found our real lives
Hidden in the truth and lies
Looking for your sense of peace
I finally found our last release.

I'm stuck in a spiral
Of death and decay
I'm sinking in deeper

Than ever today
Somebody needs me
Somebody new
I'm running away from
My past and from you.

Finally found our real lives
Hidden in the truth and lies
Looking for your sense of peace
I finally found our last release.

Finally found our real lives
Hidden in the truth and lies
Looking for your sense of peace
I finally found our last release.

There's something about your love
Something that makes me like new
There's something about your love
Something that keeps me close to you
Closer to you
Closer to you.

Finally found our real lives
Hidden in the truth and lies
Looking for your sense of peace
I finally found our last release.

Finally found our real lives
Hidden in the truth and lies
Looking for your sense of peace
I finally found our last release.

Precious Moments

Precious moments of our existence
Fading slowly to the blue,
One remains in its diamond cage
The moment found when I loved you.

What my mind is trying to scream,
Fierce as the burning coal,
Is the knowledge of forever,
The fate from which you saved my soul.

Death and life hung in limbo,
Looking back to see your face,
As your anguish finally ended,
I could see your awesome grace.

What my heart is yearning to scream,
Fierce as the burning coal,
Is the knowledge of forever,
The fate from which you saved my soul.

Death is life and life is death,
From corpse to resurrected life,
Now I know you'll stand beside me,
Save my soul through worldly strife.

What my soul and mouth are screaming,
Fierce as the burning coal,
Is the knowledge of forever,
The fate from which you saved my soul.

End of the Line

I don't know who I am anymore,
Just one lonely head in a sea of law,
The face that stares back from the mirror is not mine,
The station's ahead, it's the end of the line.
I don't have a clue who dies or survives,
I'm injured and dying while everyone lives their lives,
Invisible to the world where love isn't real,
But just an illusion – it's only pain that we feel.

I've hurled my phone against the wall,
It's silence is agony as nobody will call,
Where nobody cares is the place that we lose,
I'm the one on the bench that no-one will choose,
So I retreat into a shell, where I feel alive,
Safe in my mind where my thoughts take a drive,
But the world don't let me stay there for more than a day,
All I feel is pain – happiness is dragged away.

So I search for what I need, a release from it all,
I'm sick of it all and I refuse to play ball,
So give me a gun or some pills or a noose,
I want to die before all hell breaks loose.
I'm misunderstood by anyone I know,
I've been gradually sinking to lower than low.
So smile and wipe your eyes and be happy for me,
Because you are all trapped, but I'm finally free.

Message

I want to write a message. A message
Screaming, breaking, exploding out of the pen.
A message the world can read and feel, can feel
Inspired by, to take action against the world itself.

A message for the masses. A message
That stands up to world power for the little guys.
A message full of the ****your attitude towards
Politics the world is steeped in up to its neck.

A message for the world I create. A message
That speaks to the internal dimensions of the soul,
Created by the subconscious as an escape route
From the harsh realities of the physical planes.

A message saying wake up. A message
About the devastation blasted into cosy families by
The black box in the corner, showing
The truth to those who refuse to accept it.

A message shouting two small words. A message
Screaming ****you to those in control with all
The soul, a message tearing through the fibres
Of the soul like a bullet from a gun.

A message of death, the only constant in
A world of monstrosities. A message that is
A bullet, tearing through the fibres of the
Soul and the flesh, skin and bone of the skull.

I want to be a message, a message screaming,
Breaking, exploding from the gun.
A message the world can see and feel, can feel
Sickened, saddened, shocked and lost as my own soul.

The gun rests in my palms.

It is the message for me to write.
Lesson in Insanity

Standing in the bus shelter in the pouring rain, you see
Sheltered moments of the life you once knew.
Those couples who pass you, laughing at the weather
And the rain that falls from the sky in an outburst of depression.
Watch. Learn. See what you must do
To find out if there is any chance, any chance at all
For you to win her back into your arms.
For her to love you once more.
Those couples go by, peacefully, blissfully,
Unaware of all the hurt that fills this blasted heath
We call a planet. The world is a stage,
And I shall play my part as I watch from the wings.
Those couples so deep in love are so unaware –
They have no idea of what lurks around the corner.
Jealousy, bitterness, and perhaps the wild stabbing rage
That can so easily tear you apart if unexpressed.
I long to express it myself. No great
Bitterness or anger do I feel towards the world,
But a deep rage that can fly out of control,
As soon as I find the trigger.
That couple, so unaware of you following slowly, steadily,
Glowering at their laughing shoulders. They have done nothing
To offend you, except love each other.
Love is futile.
Teach them a lesson in insanity. Teach them
That love is an illusion and that it is better not to love at all.
You only end up hurt or dying, emotion cutting
As deep as the knife you now carry.

You speed up as they pause to kiss, and caress the blade more.
You remember her soft lips upon yours and your pride
And the futility carries you further forwards towards the lesson,
Where you will teach them the lesson they need to know.
Love is nothing more than an illusion, used
To tear your soul farther from your body than you would have
Thought possible. To fall in love is futile, as you will only hurt.
One way or another all love ends.
This love in front of you ends now.
You walk up to the couple and they step aside. The girl
Closest to you, she smiles gently, youth shining out of
Her eyes with all the love in the world. This love ends now.
In insanity, in grief, all love ends.
The knife makes hardly a sound as you leave it in her. You keep walking
And smile to yourself as you hear the stricken realisation
That mars the boys face.
She reminded you of your only love. Now they are both gone.
Insanity is such a hard thing once learned,
Often given, often enforced, never earned.
You understand none of this, about what drives a man to pain,
To jealousy, insanity, and to kill again.

Come What May

Never knew I could feel like this
Like I've never seen the sky before
I want to vanish inside your kiss
Everyday I love you more and more
Listen to my heart
Can you hear it sing?
Telling me to give you everything
Seasons may change
Winter to spring
But I love you until
The end of time

Come what may
Come what may
I will love you until my dying day

Suddenly the world seems
Such a perfect place
Suddenly it moves with
Such a perfect grace
Suddenly my life
Doesn't seem such a waste
But our world revolves around you
And there's no mountain too high
No river too wide
Sing out this song
I'll be there by your side
Storm clouds may gather
And stars may collide
But I love you until
The end of time.

Tom's Diary

When Tom was baptised at thirteen, someone gave him a diary as a present. This is what he wrote starting from that day – 17th December 2000. At the foot of each page was a verse which I have included along with Tom's added 'thoughts'.

17.12.00

Praise the Lord! My baptism may be over but I've got the rest of my life to live as a Christian. It is now 10:00pm and I'm writing this before I go to bed (school tomorrow!) while the experience is fresh in my mind.

It started like any other Sunday – I got up and went downstairs to watch T.V. and until I actually got dressed it felt perfectly normal. When I was dressed, the excitement set in.

We got to church at about 10:00am and I just had to run about a bit, I was so excited. When the people arrived (first up was Mathew J and Co.) I couldn't keep still. Stevie T. made it from Derbyshire, and Grandma and Grandad and Auntie Katie came too.

I went out to my group as normal, then we all went back, sang my song (My Jesus, My Saviour) and I gave my testimony. It went well but I think I rushed it a bit. Then for the baptism!

Phil read my verse (Psalm 45) – **"My heart overflows with a beautiful thought! I will recite a lovely poem to the king, for my tongue is like the pen of a skilful poet"** – And then I was dunked. I felt great! I couldn't stop smiling afterwards when Phil prayed for me. When we got home, we helped prepare for the meal afterwards, which went really well. All in all, the best day of my life!

27.12.00

God is like a small child with His favourite toy – during the day He will always be with it, talking to it and making it feel alive, even though its senses are dead compared to His.

And at night, the child cuddles up close to the toy, and they keep each other warm and give each other comfort. The child wraps his love around the toy.

We believers are that toy – God will always be with us and keep us company. At the harder and scarier times, we will feel God's presence even closer, warming us and comforting us.

8. November 2003

Well, well, well. Its three years since you last even opened this book. And how things have changed! Hey, I still believe in Jesus, but hey, life is for the living, yeah? And that's what I plan to do.

I've had a few firsts – first girlfriend, first drunken experience. I was so innocent back then.

Nirvana is such a great group. They've been my world recently: a world of heavy atmosphere. In 'You know You're Right' and 'Smells like Teen Spirit' especially, you hear their attitude, which I've adopted. They've got talent, they've got skills, but most importantly they've got experience and a **** you attitude towards the world in general.

So it may not be very Christian, but so what. Kurt Cobain was beaten raw by life, with and without, inside and outside of Nirvana and his music. So much so, he was suicidal. But he knew about life and he knew how to say **** you to the U.S.A. to the country, to the world – dammit, to the entire ******* universe. He knew how to fight back against the world that beat him down, or at least tried to. And that's what I want now. Not the whole mind**** that his life became before he died, but the rest. The experience of living life as much as I can.

I said I've already had a few firsts; maybe more are just round the corner, maybe not. But life is good and my parents are twats. I follow Kurt's way of life, no matter what they say. In my own way of course. They're too useless at punishing to think of anything decent. If they ground me, I'll walk out.

You really expect me to listen to them? **** Off, I'm my own person. Later!

T. Slough

Joy, like love, is multiplied when it is shared – bollocks – depends who you share it with!

2nd December 2003

Isn't life a mother*******bitch? #### was a slapper, ### was different – I actually loved her. And now she's gone. But hey, at least we can still be friends!

I still love her. I. Still. LOVE her! But I'm not angry, I'm pissed off yes, but not angry.

I've sort of had the usual sympathy talks from every one who doesn't really give a ****! But once again, Nirvana is my world. I didn't cry when she said goodbye, but an hour later, to the heavy drums and discordant guitar and grainy vocals of 'You know you're right' I sobbed uncontrollably my grief and anger.

Nirvana is a world, and this world I will make mine.

I've calmed down from that passionate emotion, and I do still want to be friends, the question is, how the hell will I manage? I will though, because it will be for her.

(**** that, where's the vodka?)

T. Slough

3rd/4th December 2003

After the anger comes depression, and then acceptance. I've gone through them all now, but am still lingering slightly in depression, the old feelings of futility lurking just below the surface.

I'm probably meeting ### on Saturday, it's going to be hard for me but I'll cope and be a good friend for her sake. I've always been a good actor when I want to be. And so I'll act.

A friend has been cool and has said what I've wanted to hear – that maybe there's a chance * we will get back together after exams. She said we were moving too fast. I'm guessing it was my fault. But we'll be mates, for my sake as much as hers.

PS. From the asterisk onwards, I was pissed, great fun with everyone home!

May the God of hope fill you with all joy – some ******* joy!

Disillusion

Everyone talks to me about everything,
All that's ever happened between us,
Soured by too much love as the birds sang,
Now I'm lying pissed on the school bus,
Disillusioned with love and life and death,
Wanting to know what the hell's coming now,
Agony deepens with every passing breath,
My mother********bovine cow
What the **** is love in this world?
A word but nothing more,
Out of the blue my emotions are hurled,
Abandoned I stand and knock at your door.
Will you answer? Will you run?
Leave me to starve as you save yourself?
You ******* whore is anything fun,
I can't put my feelings for you on the shelf.
Friendship is good, but not good enough,
I love you too much to leave things to luck,
You don't want to know me well sorry, but tough.
Tell it to someone who really gives a ****

I'll do what you want while I love you inside,
Act to your face and hope for the best,
I'll take what you give and hope you won't hide
You're all from me and just give me the rest.

Accept it, Tom, because it's all you have
She don't give a **** for the way that you feel,
Stop living in dreams and accept what you have
Wake up, Tom, and start living for real.

This is the last for a while. An accurate account of my thoughts while I was slightly drunk this afternoon. It's a text I wrote and nearly sent to ###; "I'm slightly pissed right now so why the hell I am I don't know. I still really love you, you know that. I really hope I don't send this 'cos I know I'll regret it. Love you more than you deserve. ****
You bitch! I can do much better than you. Maybe ###, ### really nice. I wouldn't mind boring her fine ass any day of the week. What comes next?"
Kinda cool, but kinda scary huh? I honestly didn't mean it. Honest.
Later – if I can help it, much later!
T. Slough

Peace is heaven's gift to those who share God's love. – then why do I feel peaceful now?

14th December 2003

Is it against the law of God to hate your parents? And if it is – do I care?
Not that I do of course. I get the odd moment when a carving knife up to the hilt in mumsies back looks increasingly inviting but then who doesn't?
Last Friday was ###'s first gig and a complete catalogue of everything I drank is; vodka,slivovic, metaxa, fosters and absenthe. And for the next few months I'm strictly teetotal by my own choice...My parents were considerably nice considering what I did and that they called the ambulance. And I have learned my lesson.
I've lost some of the fire you can see in the last three entries and gained some life experiences. My parents don't trust me; I don't particularly care. What I do not like however, is my mother's attempts to get me to do what she would do – the nice Christian thing.
I'm learning about life the only way you can really learn – the hard way. If she doesn't like it then fine but I will learn my way. She cannot force me. If I want to stay on my own Sunday nights then so be it because I am my own person. I'm still a Christian but God did not instruct us to worship Him by going to church twice a week on Sundays. I follow Him my way, as I think I can. And if mother don't understand then fine. She's never understood me anyway, just because I am not my brother. She doesn't even try – I remember countless occasions when

she twisted my words to make it sound like something she would say if it was me.

Only God knows me better than I do, and He knows I am not my mother.

T. Slough

I AM GOING TO SHOOT MYSELF. If I am to die, it will be suicide, from a gun.

T. Slough

9th January 2004

They still don't listen to me do they? I try to say one tiny thing but mother takes it completely the wrong way and we both end up getting extremely annoyed with each other. Whatever happens she blames it all on my music, my bands – whatever the hell she can to make sure she is not to blame.

It's that invisibility factor again isn't it? The fact that you are only seen when people want to see you or you draw attention to yourself. Otherwise you're invisible and inaudible. I sometimes feel like screaming, yelling – anything to get the attention I feel I need to survive.

And without it? Without it I'll just have to draw attention to myself. One last time. go out with a bang, literally.

I don't want to hurt anyone but me. I just want to make them realise who I am, what I am and even why I am who I am. If it takes my death to do that then so be it. And if all that happens is five minutes grief and a newspaper headline, so be it.

I have no credit on my phone and not enough time to use the landline. I can't talk to my parents. I can't talk to anyone except ### because he is the only one who knows how I feel. I feel trapped, inescapably backed down a narrow alleyway with no way out and the immortal darkness closing in from all sides. The only way out is to die. To shoot myself.

My parents don't understand me, they never even try to, they blame everything on my music, my bands, everything that is my life. They never will understand me.

They've had enough chances to understand, to stop me before I go too fat. They have done NOTHING.

They can't stop me shooting myself, nothing can.

T. Slough

I wonder if the band's lyrics spoke to me so much tonight and made me feel like I did is because ### wrote a lot of them, and he feels the same as I do?

I'm glad I talked to him tonight; I just hope he can trust me enough to talk to me if he ever needs to. God knows, I'll probably need to talk to him again sometime and I hope he won't like, brush me off and will actually be the friend I need.

But the one thing I can never, NEVER tell him is about how I feel for ### because it would probably spell the end for both of us – bang bang, you know?

I don't know if he's a good actor or a convincing liar, but he seems to have shared the same emotions as me. Maybe I'm just deluding myself, trying to tell myself I'm not alone in this oppressive darkness that permeates to my very soul, but it's nice to think someone knows how I feel.

9th December 2003
Diary of My Mind

In this bleak universe I have created, I stand for nothing as nothing but a blind depressed, oppressed rage that builds inside my chest, threatening to burst out at any moment. Can I control it? Can I control myself?

No.

It is the hardest thing in the world for me not to scream, to shout a long horrible endless stream of curses and swear words towards my friends, my family, my teachers...to the entire world.

You can have no idea how I feel, because you are not me. No-one has any idea what the hell I am going through, not even me.

It's almost as if I'm two or three different people. The first is you at school, having fun but desperately insecure and trying to prove myself as worthy of my friends. A bit of a loser really, getting drunk to prove yourself to everyone, including yourself.

The second is you at home and church, a charming, upright member of the local young community, who helps those both older and younger than him. You are completely different, never swearing and always on the best of behaviour – a creep, fawning up and playing at being grown up.

Then there's the real me, the person writing this. I'm the internal primal emotion and feelings that surface whenever others are around in more moderate levels. I'm the one who only really comes out when I'm alone, with a pen or keyboard to write with and Nirvana and alcohol to inspire me to write things like this. An account of my real feelings, even now.

I'm in a sort of climb-a-clock-tower-with-an-uzi sort of mood, wanting to scream ****!!! At the top of my voice. Know what I mean? All because of ### and the death of the person I was because of her, my other personality who is now dead and not quite forgotten, and won't be for a long time, who's showing in everyone else but especially the real me here, making me feel like crawling into a dark corner and curl up and either die or cry my eyes out.

If only the real me was capable of expression, and not the wooden featureless nothing that the bastard of a creator has made me into. Yes. I am meaning this. I don't give a s*** anymore about God – he don't care about me, so why should I care about him? He's just a giant sadistic ****** who gives us good things and takes them away to laugh at our pain, like a kid on an anthill with a magnifying glass. He don't give a s*** about us, up there on the cloud. Jesus was a w ****** and if He was the Son of God then I'm going straight to hell and don't give a s***.

**** Christ, man. I'm converting.

Added on 1st January 2004

The person I describe there lives on in my soul but not so violently. My life has become one unending river of pain and emotion. The real me writing all these is incapable of expressing emotion but very much can he feel it. I burn with depression, anger, jealousy and love…

And strangely enough it's this last emotion, the one that should bring most relief from pain that brings most of the pain itself. Why?

Because of who I love. I can't help it but I love ###. I love her so desperately she is killing me whenever she touches, or kisses or even talks to her boyfriend with that loving, eternal expression shining out of her eyes towards him.

Let's face it; I'm a loser whatever happens here. If they split up I'd have a slight chance of telling her how I feel and even less chance of her returning it, but still more chance than I have at the moment. But to me, they epitomise what love is and if they split up, any belief I hold onto that love still exists in this hellish world would be shattered and I would just sink deeper into depression than I am now. Either way, I lose.

And what would I lose? Would that be the final straw that broke the proverbial donkeys back? The one thing I have clear in my mind is that my life will be ended with a bullet.

I'm talking about suicide, people.

Are you as shocked as my parents will be if they ever read this? Because I sure as hell would be. Anyone other than who saw my death would be shocked, saying that I had no reason. I have my reasons all right, it's just this emotionless face that I am forced to wear by my God means that I can't show them to anyone.

All I lack is the gun.

Coming from the mind of one so young as I, this shouldn't be so hard to understand. Neither is it anything but my appraisal of life before my death.

Life is about pain. You go from heartache to heartbreak, each time sinking deeper into the emptiness your soul creates from depression, your soul dies, and then you die. Simple as that.

True, there are islands of happiness, relationships and the like. But these only end, causing more pain, or cause pain in other ways. Even if you find 'the one' and marry her, there will still be rows and more pain and emptiness.

People will try to fill this emptiness, to forget it with women and drugs and alcohol and fame. But all they find is that these are empty too.

The only thing that fills the emptiness is God. All life leads to death and the only way to you can see God's face is by dying.

So to end it all. I am not writing this just before suicide, only because I lack the means. To end an empty life, leave an empty hole in the skull. I will shoot myself. And may God judge me as he sees fit.

T. Slough

To try and coherently order my thoughts and feelings into a form the rest of the world could understand would take much more than this torn out centerpage would allow. But let's do what we can to understand the hell inside my mind.

You probably already know I want to die. That is a fact as much a feeling, that when I die I will shoot myself. I always feared growing old – to die young in search of ultimate happiness is better than to live without joy into old age and feebleness and dementia. But maybe this is a form of dementia – the madness I have inflicted upon myself that I should so desperately want to end everything.

 NO. This madness is another sort – love. I am so desperately madly depressingly suicidal because of a forbidden love. I can't help loving her. God knows I've tried to stop loving her and this dilemma is what is driving me to my doom.

I love her and I want her so much it hurts like a bullet itself but maybe its not ### I want but what she has with ### – love. If what they have ended then I would be that much closer to death because I would know the thing I wanted most was a lie.

So maybe I can achieve it with someone else? Not likely. When I was with ### I worried so much and she seems to have started the whole suicide thing off – with unknown help from ### of course.

*******hell, I'm an idiot. Why should I ever believe that I deserve a bit of love from other humans? God loves me and – no offense big guy – so ******* what? I feel His love but no-one else's and that's why I need to die. When I am dead I will be able to physically see the only one whose love I can feel.

The only thing I am worried about is what is causing this depression on a spiritual front. I've always believed in demons – am I possessed by some?

I can never know the answer to this until I am dead or they leave me. But then again, I always had a good imagination. Maybe I'm borrowing this all from the things I know, mainly Kurt Cobain, the man who's music drove him to put a bullet in his skull like my writings and tortured imaginings are driving me. Maybe that's where the idea for a gun came into my mind or maybe the entire depressing feelings are a romantic idealistic lifestyle that I'm inventing subconsciously to make me feel like my life is worth something, that my death might be for some unknown cause or martyrdom, glorifying death so my life may amount to something, even if that something is a funeral and newspaper headline.

Bulls***. All complete and utter bulls***! If any of that fantasy crap was true then why would I have written it down like that? The only real explanations are that I do really want to die or I am possessed.

It's funny really, how you do all these letters to no-one to explain how you feel and then never show them to anyone! Is it just to keep that penchant for death fresh in your mind, or just because you're a useless conversationalist. I wouldn't be surprised if no-one missed you. Sure they'd cry at first but only from shock. I bet that just one day after the funeral they'd all feel really glad that that annoying, pathetic little s*** isn't around anymore to follow them round and attempt humour.

Shut up inner voice of patheticism! I don't need you anymore. You lie, cheat and stab my soul in an attempt to make me feel bad. Not anymore. If I die it's my own goddam choice.

AND I CHOOSE TO DIE

–*"You try and block me out, don't you? You try to shut me out so you don't have to hear what I have to say to you that could make or break your life"*–

–*"I shut you out as much as possible because I don't want to hear what you have to say! I try to hide from you, to drown out your voice with the created world in my mind that is familiar and comforting, but all you do is shout that little bit louder and refuse to let me shut the door on you."*

I DON'T WANT TO HEAR WHAT YOU HAVE TO SAY. You do not know what's best for me – you are neither God nor my conscience. You are an arrogant, belittling voice that permeates my every thought in one way or another. It is you that has led me to wanting to die, and yet it is not to make you happy that I will kill myself. It will be for my own sake that I will pull the trigger, not yours. It will be so that I will never have to hear your voice again.

And so I don't have to live in this world anymore.

T. Slough

Tonight is the closest I have come in a long time to hanging myself. Or overdosing, or doing whatever it takes to kill myself without backing out. It's certainly the longest I've spent curled up since that day. I just couldn't move and it's the closest I've come to tears of despair since this whole dam thing started.

And why? Because I am jealous, insanely jealous of ###. I can't help it. I know I shouldn't be jealous – for some reason he is more screwed up than I am – but I cannot help it. All because I love ###

It sounds ridiculous if I say it out loud, but I can't help loving her, believe me I've tried not to. And this latest fit of despair is all because of an image I hold, of them lying together, her head on his chest, his hand idly stroking her hair…

This picture is driving me closer to the edge than anything else I have ever known, and believe me it's scary. The one thing I want is to die, preferably by shooting myself.

I have seriously thought about shooting myself at school, probably at the end of our Drama practical exam. After all, life is nothing more than a stage… wouldn't it be ironic if life ended on one in front of the girl who's driving me mad because she will never be mine?

All I need's to get hold of a gun.

T. Slough

The closest I've come to dying was last night when I nearly hung myself and the same again tonight. It wasn't like I planned it but it happened.

"Smells like Teen Spirit" on the C.D. played (one of the songs I said I'd kill myself to, along with *"Stacked Actors"* and *"Lonely as You,"* by Foofighters, *"Around the World"* and *"Can't Stop"* by Chilli Peppers, *"You Held the World in Your Arms"* and *"American English"* or *"Scottish Fiction"* by Idlewild and *"You Know You're Right"* by Nirvana) and the bootlace lying there real handy on the bed. No long note beforehand, no tears, no nothing. I just tied it into a noose, tied it onto the hook on the back of the door, put it around my neck and knelt down. If I hadn't tied it too long I probably wouldn't have stopped myself.

But I did, only because I didn't want my death to hurt so much. The fact I repeated it again earlier tonight means the thought is still there, if not the heart. That's why I need to shoot myself — because otherwise I will not die.

Last night was done almost in a trance, tonight was in earnest and the only reason I couldn't go through with it was because I lack the courage.

says he is depressed but what possible reason does he have to feel depressed? He knows his friends are his friends. I don't and constantly feel insecure. He has the most perfect girlfriend in the world. I don't and I have no-one that I can love as he loves her. He has EVERYTHING I ever wanted from life, whereas I have nothing. And he's depressed.

I don't hate him, and I would like him to get better. He's the only person who can understand how I feel because he goes through it himself.

I love ### and there's nothing I can do about it. But I swear that if he hurts her in any way, I will make him pay. I'll kill him.

And then join him in hell myself.

Maybe not, but the message behind the threat is real enough. If he hurt her in any way I would want him to pay. Out of my feelings related elsewhere for them as a couple I would kill myself. No cowardice. The noose or overdose or whatever the hell it took would be what I needed. A gun would be preferable but if I can't die how I want, I'll die another way.

The noose is still on the back of the door, maybe next time I will use it, and it will be for real.

T. Slough

When I was Seven and Eight

When I was seven and eight, I read a lot. Any book that I could find, but my favourites were fantasy. What were, to my young self, huge works of epic battles and mystic heroes.

When I was nine and ten, I watched a lot of films. Anything on the television but my favourites was still fantasy. The battles, the heroes who always saved the day and got the girl.

When I was eleven and twelve, I read more. Anything that grabbed my attention, from fantasy to fact to comedy. My mind drank it all in and my world began to develop into a shell of what it is now.

When I was thirteen and fourteen, I watched more films. The battles fed my bloodlust; the romance filled my mind with an idealistic universe I foolishly thought was like real life.

And now, at fifteen and sixteen, I come out of my created world and realise that real life is nothing like what I imagined. I find myself unable to cope, unable to survive without withdrawing into the imaginings I know and believe should be real. I find myself still wanting the epic stories to be true, in my life and everyone else's. I find my bloodlust dulling for any blood that is fake; that I know doesn't create pain and fear but only a nasty mess on the set floor. I find myself hungering more and more for the guns on screen, for the bullets to be real rounds of deadly ammunition.

And I find myself hungering yet more and more for all the guns, all the swords and bows and axes and weapons of destruction that have so already destroyed the shell that my mind has become. I hunger for all of those weapons to be pointing directly at my fragile skull.

And I find myself screaming for them to fire, to blow an empty hole in an empty skull, to blast the delirious rantings of a fevered imagination from my head and end it all.

I cannot cope in the real world. I cannot cope in my false world. If I cannot live in either, I will live in neither.

The bullets will all fire. It's only a matter of time.

22nd January 2004

Letters that Tom wrote to Alan, James and Myself

Mum, Dad, James – Thanks for Everything!

Maybe the reason I told you none of this before is because I didn't want to be talked out of it. Maybe I've just felt I couldn't talk to you or couldn't find the right words or anything that could really describe my feelings.

If you must know, this is my third suicide. Those red marks on my neck earlier, just after Christmas? I'd tried to hang myself. Now I feel so bad I can't keep going.

Don't blame it on anything other than myself, not my friends, not my music, nothing. This is all my own fault, all down to my own feelings of an inability to cope in the real world and having to retreat to my almost perfect fairytale imaginings.

I can't really explain it here. On my bed is a diary of sorts that does a better job. All I can tell you now is that I can't go on in this world and the sooner I meet God the better.

Thanks. Don't cry – I'll see you later!

Love you forever,
Tom

To My Ever –Loving Parents

You have been nicer to me than I have ever deserved and maybe that's what love is, so do me one last thing and don't cry.

I don't feel I ever really knew love, except for from God. I'm probably wrong but it feels like my mind just became so screwed up I couldn't think past the end of a gun. Maybe if I had, it wouldn't have come to this.

But let's face it; I never was exactly normal, was I? I never felt like I fitted in, despite what everyone told me and I needed to feel that, and never did.

Mum, I know what you will do. You'll blame it all on my music, my friends, probably even yourself – in fact on every person who is not me. Don't, this whole issue is about me and my inability to cope with growing old.

I've never feared death because I've known I'll go heaven. What I have feared is old age and dementia; only, unlike Peter Pan, I can't stay young.

The world is hell, I realise that. But it never seemed to live up to even the lowest standards I could set and maybe it's this that's led me close to the edge, so all I had to do was tilt over.

Two things I ask of you last of all – firstly, read my file on suicide to get a better grip on my feelings. Second, get the large envelope of letters to my friends at school. Thanks.

I love you forever. Don't be sad,

Your son,
Tom XXX

Letters Tom Wrote to his Friends

We felt it right at the time not to pass these on and as I re-write them here, I shall omit any names. As Tom had tried to take his life on a previous occasion, there are sometimes two letters to the same people, as with the letters he wrote to us.

"I remember you saying that you'd shared a lot of my feelings, depression, suicidalness (not a word, but hey, whatcha gonna do?) And the feelings of no self worth. I also remember you saying after you asked if how I felt was anything to do with you, that if it was then you'd probably kill yourself or words to that effect.

Don't, my killing myself and the emotions that have led up to it, are nothing to do with you, and you have a hell of a lot more to live for before you die.

Myself, I feel that life has already become too much to handle. It's not stress and an inability to cope with all the work so much as a bitter jaded disappointed pain inside me that the world hasn't lived up to any of my expectations, low as I seem to have set them.

So hey, don't cry for me. I'm a Christian right? If God forgives me for killing myself, I'm already in Paradise while you're stuck on a ******up hole we call Earth. I'd like to think that my death will prompt you to undergo a bit of soul-searching, maybe read the Bible and come to know and recognise Jesus and His great love for you as I know it. But

I'm a realist, and you're more likely to have a screaming ranting rage at the heavens and disown all knowledge of knowing God how He wants to know you. Ah well.

So sleep easy and don't have nightmares. I never wanted this to cause you guys any pain. I love you all too much and you don't deserve that because you've all been such great friends to me.

Remember my life, not my death.

Love you. Sluff."

"You're a great kid. Keep on going.

That's pretty much all I have to say to you, other than an explanation. I don't know if I am depressed or just disillusioned but I really can't cope anymore with the daily routine of living. It's become too much of an effort. That's all you need to know.

Look after yourself – I would hate for you to do something stupid like I have. You are in no way guilty – no-one is except for me.

Have a good life.

Sluff."

"The first thing that I ask is that you keep this private, unless you feel everyone else needs to see it. The second is you don't think me mad. I'll be blunt. I love you and have done since I've known you, and still do in my final sleep. You can have no idea how much you've torn me apart every time you touch or kiss or hold ###, (boyfriend) especially after ### (Tom's girlfriend) – it's not your fault. And I would never blame any of this on you or want to hurt you.

How have I loved you? That's what's been confusing me and tearing me apart. I love you as a person – let's face it, you're perfect. I've wanted you for so long it's become just a dull ache. But I've wanted you to be happy, like whenever you're with ###, and these two emotions have torn my soul apart like …well, like a bullet.

But it goes further, I've loved what you have with ###. This is harder to explain – especially since ###, you two have become the embodiment of love to me. Therefore if you two split up, it would be like what I thought love was – actually didn't exist.

I don't know, maybe I've watched too many films. But I know my

heart, which is why I know I love you and why I know I want to die.
So stay how I remember you. Stay happy, smiling, loving unreservedly.
You probably never worried about what I thought anyway, but I'm no
longer around even if you did.

I love you so much it hurts more than the gun. Don't feel guilty
because my death is nothing to do with you – it's all about me and how
I can't handle my mind.

I love you. I love you. I love you.

Sluff'

"You are the last person I will write to; because you are the one I have
most to say to. Please keep this personal unless you think everyone else
needs to see it.

There's no easy way to say this – you've been tearing me apart inside
for ages. Every time you've brushed against me or been with ### and
so madly in love with him in front of me has been agony. I love you. I
love you and have done so for a very long time.

I don't want you to feel guilty in any way. I love you and so it has been
painful to see you with ###, but it's my own fault it's come to this.
I'm just messed up in the head, simple as that. I haven't been able to
cope with the real world since I came to Chipping Campden school,
and now at 16 I've finally come to hate it and realise I cant continue in
it. It's too full of pain and misery for me to want to continue living in
it.

I've always had a good imagination, ever since I started reading, and
maybe that's been my problem. Maybe I had too high expectations of
life to be able to cope with the reality, but hey, that's what life is.

Look after ### – you two are a great couple. Don't let him do
anything stupid just because I have.

Please don't cry. I want to remember you as happy.

I love you. I love you. I love you. I love you. I love you.

For ever.

Sluff'

" Just want to say how you've all been the best friends you possibly
could be. I love you all, you've been great to me – better than I've
deserved. I just don't want to live in this hell of a world anymore. It's
no-one's fault, I've just never been able to cope in this reality,
emotionally or physically.

So stay good guys, and don't be too sad for me. I've set myself free.

Love you all loads.
Sluff'"

As I have been retyping these words of Tom's, I have been trying to read them from an objective view and not as his mother but that's been hard to do, as they have retouched chords and nerves that I maybe have tried to bury. It was all so desperately sad and so very avoidable if only Tom had felt able to share even some of his thoughts but even when he gave us a particular poem (No Regrets for instance) when he was crying out for help to deal with what was in his mind, he could not begin to start and I could not begin to imagine, as outwardly he was the Tom we knew and loved.

So how to end this on a positive note?

I remember giving all that Tom had written to our G.P. and as he read them he was convinced that Tom would have been schizophrenic by his early twenties or at least quite mentally unwell. I don't know if that was a great help or not. It was and still is a comfort to know that he has not had to go through all that that entails but was it just simply part of growing up — let's face it, we've all been where Tom was in the unrequited love stakes at some point in our lives and we none of us felt the need to end it all but for him, it consumed him. Would things have sorted themselves out if he had given it more time? — in absolutely no way do I apportion any blame whatsoever to the people Tom wrote about. All blame must and does rest solely with Tom for being unable to share his feelings and with us as his family for not recognising anything at all of what he was going through.

I tried to be encouraging and supportive whenever I saw a need and to try to help him talk about his feelings but as you've read, it wasn't good enough. It wasn't what he wanted to hear and it actually annoyed him. I guess I probably would have been the same with my mum. It's that 'parent thing' where you think they have no idea what you are thinking or feeling because they cannot possibly have felt anything like it because they were never young — they were just always your parents, having landed from planet Zod and never having experienced life at all!

I find it difficult to talk to my own parents – or for them to talk to me. Not sure which way round it is, but I think it is a generation thing, whereby they weren't close to their own parents and so it goes on down the generations. Alan has said it was the same for him. He cannot remember talking in depth with his parents about anything that mattered. I envy those families that do have that relationship but for us it hasn't been that way. I have always struggled when my sister and I are together with my parents – I always feel insecure and insignificant compared to her – very much the little sister. She and my mum's relationship is much more talkative and mum shares much more with my sister than she ever would with me. Is that a younger sibling thing? I guess I talked more with James, about what was going on in our family, day to day stuff, especially when Alan was away working. Did that affect Tom?

Alan and I were just thinking these things through and realising that it goes much wider than just your immediate family. We would say that we are 'rubbish' at conversation beyond the 'how are you', the weather, work and family. We are happier in our own company than in the company of others – because it is easier, not because we don't like people! What example does that set for our children? How much does that rub off unknowingly? How many years can you get away with thinking you are shy (or 'reserved') and not put the effort into making yourself talk to people – and it is an effort.

I know that we are much better people and more able to converse and hold relationships since we became Christians – but by choice we would still surround ourselves with those lovely people for whom talking and chatting is as natural as breathing, so that we don't have to be seen to dry up and be stuck for words.

So how much that had an influence upon Tom I don't know. You have read my journal and know how hard I found it to share with anyone. It was the same for him but at least we have a good idea of how he felt and why he couldn't go on living. However much we long to have him back, however much we may think it all such a shame and a waste, and however much we would do anything to have changed things, it still happened. He still killed himself. He is still no longer here and we have to go on living with that fact that he chose to die.

Our one consolation I suppose is that through the reading of this book, others will be helped. Families may be able to talk more openly. People suffering from depression will seek help. Parents will view their own relationships with their own children differently and place more importance and emphasis on being open and honest and talking more from their hearts about where they are at, what worries them, what scares them about life and growing up, and relationships with boy/girlfriends and the whole different ball-game that that is with hormones and teenage pressures etc.

If you have read this through to the end – please be encouraged and uplifted. Please see that we are still here, still giving thanks and praise to the God who has carried us and who wouldn't let this book go. Please see that there is so much life at the end of our tunnel, so much more for us to do and if you have identified with anything within its pages, hold on, keep holding on. Seek help, talk to someone who will listen and you too, will see the light at the end of your dark tunnel and will come through into the glorious sunshine of life with meaning and purpose. But you have to take the first step…

I will say that now…. there are people with whom I feel I can share my deepest thoughts, my worries, my insecurities, people who maybe were not in my life a few years ago but whom God has brought into my orbit – and maybe that is why I could share with them because I did not know them before Tom died. Who knows? But I am grateful for their unconditional love and honesty.

But above all I encourage you to seek Jesus as your Saviour. He loves you with a passion that will never burn out, with an understanding that no-one can fathom, and He is who He says He is – the Son of the living God. He is not a crutch for when you are feeling weak and needy, for when bad things happen – because they will – that's life – but He is always there, by your side, your closest friend and confidant. I am so thankful that Tom knew Him and that Tom is with Him and that we shall all be together one day, when it won't matter what Tom did or why, but that we shall just spend eternity together. That is what I live for, that is where my hope is.

What about you?

Jackie and Alan are available for speaking engagements and presentations both nationally and internationally. They also welcome visitors to their tearoom in the picturesque Cotswolds.

Jackie & Alan Slough

The Old Bakery Tearooms

4 Fountain Court, Digbeth Street

Stow on the Wold

Glos GL54 1BN

Tel: 01451 832172

E Mail: alanslough@btinternet.com

Web: www.losingtomfindinggrace.co.uk